I0188746

IMAGES
of America

DARLINGTON
COUNTY

The Darlington oak or laurel oak (*Quercus hemisphaerica*) is a variety of oak tree indigenous to an area of 120 square miles in the eastern section of Darlington County. In fertile soil, the Darlington oak is a fast-growing tree, providing beauty and shade in 10 to 20 years. This particularly venerable tree stood near the Darlington Armory for more than 150 years. In the 1940s, the U.S. Forest Service measured its height at 102 feet, with a limb spread of 100 feet and a trunk circumference of 20 feet. This image of the Darlington oak was captured by Maj. T. S. Lucas around 1900 and shows a horse and buggy pausing for a rest in the cool shade. (Courtesy of Darlington County Historical Commission archives.)

ON THE COVER: Six Darlington County gentlemen enjoy a congenial moment on the front steps of the L. E. Carrigan Store in Society Hill around 1912. From left to right are E. W. Carrigan, John E. Sumner, J. W. Grigg, L. E. Carrigan, George Snow, and "Captain" Lantham. The various four-legged pals remain anonymous. (Courtesy of Darlington County Historical Commission archives.)

IMAGES
of America

DARLINGTON COUNTY

Mary Anne Hamblen

ARCADIA
PUBLISHING

Copyright © 2008 by Mary Anne Hamblen
ISBN 978-1-5316-3391-2

Published by Arcadia Publishing
Charleston SC, Chicago IL, Portsmouth NH, San Francisco CA

Library of Congress Catalog Card Number: 2007941407

For all general information contact Arcadia Publishing at:
Telephone 843-853-2070
Fax 843-853-0044
E-mail sales@arcadiapublishing.com
For customer service and orders:
Toll-Free 1-888-313-2665

Visit us on the Internet at www.arcadiapublishing.com

This book is dedicated to the Darlington County Historical Commission and to the memory of Horace Fraser Rudisill, whose efforts to collect, document, and conserve the county's historical materials were vital to the preservation of Darlington County's cultural heritage for generations to come.

The images displayed in Darlington County *are courtesy of the Darlington County Historical Commission archives.*

CONTENTS

ACKNOWLEDGMENTS

My deepest gratitude extends to Doris G. Gandy and Kay Williamson of the Darlington County Historical Commission archives for sharing with me their time, wisdom, and extensive knowledge of Darlington County history. This book would surely not have been possible without them. *Darlington County* would also not have been realized without the expertise and unending patience of my editor at Arcadia Publishing, Maggie Bullwinkel. And to my dear family who did not like but accepted my long hours hunched over the computer, I am indebted.

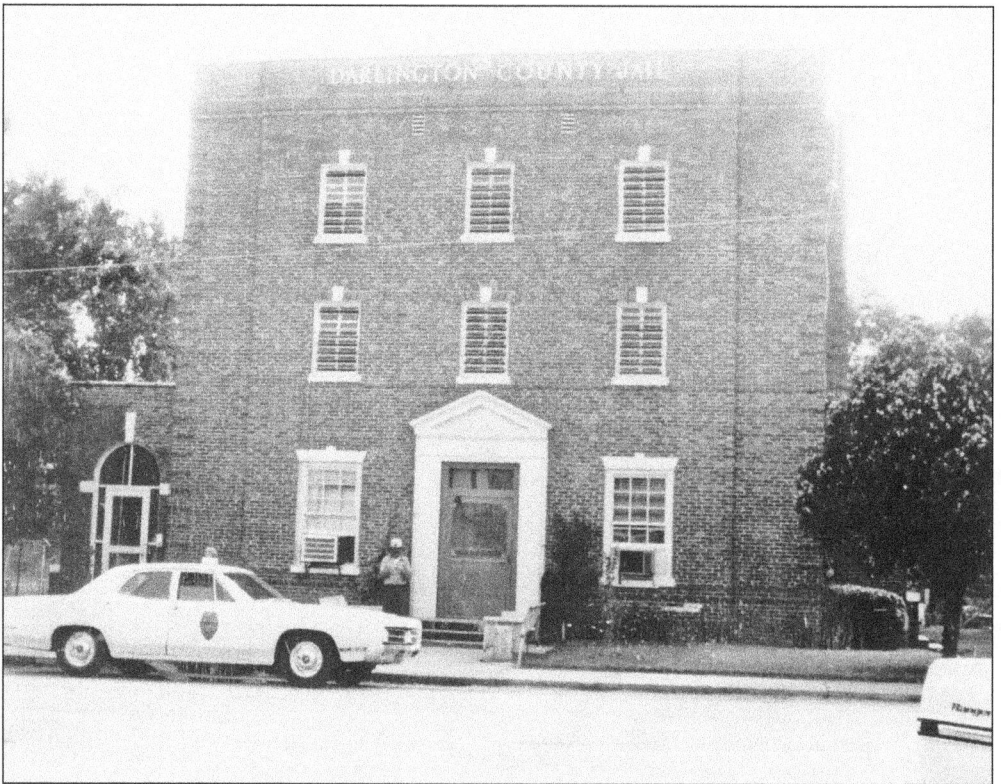

A legislative act created the Darlington County Historical Commission in 1965, an extension of the Darlington Historical Society originating in the 1930s. The historical commission occupied a room in the county courthouse until the 1980s, when the vacant county jail was renovated and made available as a repository. The building, pictured here in the 1970s, was built in 1937.

INTRODUCTION

Before settlers came to what is now Darlington County, a few small tribes of Native Americans, some Catawba but mostly Cheraw, inhabited the dense pine forests of the South Carolina backcountry, hunting among the trees and fishing from the banks of the meandering ribbon of the Pee Dee River. Welsh Baptists from Delaware were the first settlers to venture into the old Cheraw District, lured by the promise of generous land tracts along both sides of the Pee Dee granted by the British Colonial government in 1736 and 1737. The goal was to populate the backcountry wilderness.

In the early days of British royal crown rule, South Carolina was divided into parishes. Before the area became known as Darlington County in 1868, it was known as Darlington District, and before 1798, it was part of the old Cheraw District. Over those formative years, the county's edges were stretched, cut, and redefined, sometimes gaining territory and sometimes losing land, such as in the 1888 creation of Florence County to the south, and again in 1901, when Lee County formed to the east. Today Darlington County is sandwiched between the Lynches River on the east and the Pee Dee on the west and bordered by Chesterfield, Marlboro, Florence, and Lee Counties. Although it is not certain how Darlington County received its name, some speculate that it honors the distinguished Col. Henry Dixson Darlington, a hero of the Revolutionary War.

The Welshmen founded the Baptist Church of Christ in 1738 as the center of their community. The settlement known as Welsh Neck developed on a bend in the Pee Dee just across from what is now the town of Society Hill. Beginning their new lives as farmers, some of the settlers raised livestock; others planted wheat, hemp, and indigo. The river provided fish, and the forests offered plentiful beavers, deer, opossums, and squirrels. The pioneers worked to clear the land acre by acre, and their labors paid off; a few fortunes were eventually made on the river.

As the years passed, German, Swedish, Scotch Irish, English, and French settlers joined the original Welsh frontiersmen. Long Bluff, later Society Hill, was the first village in Darlington District, continuing as the hub of the area until Darlington Court House became the seat around 1900.

The American Revolution tragically impacted the backcountry. Allegiances were divided, and tempers flared between Tories and Whigs even before the official onset of battle. During the war, property was destroyed and numerous lives lost, but in typical backcountry fashion, Darlingtonians mustered courage and looked to the future.

Competition from other Southern states and persistently poor yields caused indigo, tobacco, and wheat production to flag. By the early 1800s, short-staple cotton, its processing made cost effective by the cotton gin, became the mainstay of the backcountry economy, powered by the labor of enslaved African Americans. As the cotton market created wealthy planters, demand and expansion required ever more labor. The U.S. Census of 1850 reveals that almost twice as many African Americans lived in Darlington County than whites by the mid-19th century.

From the first Welsh settlement, the South Carolina backcountry maintained a unique and separate personality from coastal residents. Sometimes this meant taking care of concerns without the blessing of the Colonial government. When trouble in the form of horse thieves and cattle rustlers plagued the region's dwellers in the 1760s, Darlingtonians took matters into their own hands and formed a vigilante group, the Regulators. The Regulator movement raised eyebrows among Lowcountry elites, but Charles Towne authorities eventually recognized the backcountry's attempt to quell outlaw activity.

In the following century, the Civil War spared Darlington County the worst of the carnage but not the aftermath, and financial and human loss fell heavily upon the area. Many native sons set out to fight; some returned with missing limbs, many not at all. The James Kelley family of Kelley-Town saw six brave sons off to war, but only two returned home. African American soldiers sacrificed as well. Henry "Dad" Brown (1830–1907), a free African American, enlisted in the Confederate army in 1861, serving as a drummer in Company H, 21st South Carolina Infantry.

Darlington County withstood another furor in the early 1890s, when a State Dispensary Board was established, allowing only one dispenser in each county to sell liquor. When a group of constables arrived in Darlington to seize illegal spirits, independence-loving citizens were involved in an altercation later named the Dispensary War. At the time, the governor declared Darlington and Florence Counties to be in a state of rebellion. Militia units responded, and although the matter was settled, the incident polished the backcountry's reputation for self-reliance and pluck.

The cotton market failed in the 20th century, dashing fortunes and hopes. Tobacco production sprouted in the fields of the county, proving lucrative for some but requiring backbreaking work from many, black planters and white alike. By the time the stock market crashed in 1929, Darlingtonians had already known hardship and economic depression.

Two world wars framed the Great Depression, and the county's young men were called to duty twice. After World War II, Darlington County embraced the nation's fetish with the automobile, unveiling the Darlington Raceway in 1950 and welcoming thousands of racing enthusiasts to the Southern 500. Celebrity and entertainment were not far behind, and a number of national personalities from Pres. Jimmy Carter to Alan Hale Jr. of *Gilligan's Island* fame graced the yearly parade and Miss South Carolina contest.

Agriculture slipped in dominance after mid-century, and some industries relocated in the 1970s. Many Darlingtonians faced poverty and unemployment as a result. Longtime activist and county councilwoman Wilhelmina P. Johnson aggressively addressed the issue of poverty in 1975, creating the Darlington County Cultural Realism Complex, Inc., with the goal of alleviating ignorance and easing impoverishment. Other facets of the Cultural Realism project were the Darlington County Historical Museum of Ethnic Culture, established to preserve and share the rich African American history Darlington County holds, and the installation of historic markers commemorating notable black citizens.

Despite the daily toil of survival and the volatility of conflict years, Darlingtonians invariably found time for merriment. Hunting, fishing, and swimming occupied free hours, and picnics, fairs, maypole dances, and traveling vaudeville shows thrilled and entertained generations, providing many happy recollections.

Darlington, Hartsville, Society Hill, Lamar, and many other communities in the county hum with daily life in the new millennium, each with its own flavor and particular memories. This book is a story about a place with swaying southern pines, Darlington oaks, and the same breathtaking crescent moon that Native Americans gazed at in the sky. Darlington County exists today through the efforts, trials, and successes of the people that made their homes in the South Carolina backcountry. In the end, this story of Darlington County is about people.

One

DARLINGTON

Darlington served as the county seat since "Darlington Courthouse" appeared on the map in the early 1900s. For Southern novelist William Gilmore Simms in 1843, "the village of Darlington was a small neat town, with a handsome brick Court House, a jail, sundry taverns, etc." Schools and churches form the heart of a community, but a courthouse speaks most eloquently to civic spirit and pride. Local lore recounts a disagreement over the location of the first courthouse. According to Alexander Gregg in *History of the Old Cheraws*, "Col. Lamuel Benton wanted it built at Mechanicsville and Capt. Elias DuBose wanted it located at Cuffey Town. . . . In a compromise, they agreed to ride on horseback, starting from their respective communities, towards each other and that the court house be built at the spot where they met." The two converged at a crossroads on the property of John King, who subsequently donated the land for the courthouse and adjacent lots.

By 1818, Darlington Village flourished, and the Darlington Society established the Darlington Academy to educate local youth. A new brick courthouse was erected in the town square in 1825, and by the 1830s, churches for Darlington Presbyterians, Baptists, and Methodists emerged. Pearl Street hummed as the focal point for activity in the 1870s. The Darlington Manufacturing Company, a cotton mill, opened its doors in 1885 and heralded a surge in new industry. The company was joined in the 1890s by the Darlington Phosphate Company, the Darlington Compress Company, a marble works, and a canning factory. Waterworks and electric power served Darlington at the beginning of the 20th century.

Ground was broken in 1901 for a spectacular town hall–opera house designed by Columbia architect Frank P. Milburn. A courthouse designed by Darlington native William A. Edwards graced the town square in 1904.

The post–World War II building boom launched a new era and included the construction of the Darlington Raceway in 1950. The old cotton mill closed in 1956, but other industry arrived, such as Nucor Steel in 1968 and a Celanese plant in 1973. Darlington County today remains a strong player in South Carolina's economy and counts tourism as a vital enterprise.

The 1825 Darlington courthouse was destroyed by fire in 1866, and a new building was constructed on its foundation in 1873 with a similar design, pictured here shortly after completion. A tower with a fire bell was added later. County offices were housed in the building until 1903, when they were relocated to other spaces in the square, and this building was demolished in preparation for the construction of a newer courthouse.

The Darlington town square has long been the hub for town activity. This photograph was taken around 1900 on Pearl Street looking east. A shopper secures his horse and wagon, perhaps in town for a meal at one of the local restaurants and to stock up on groceries at the E. F. Stevenson Grocery Store. On the left is the Darlington Café and Early's Hardware Store.

Renowned architect Frank P. Milburn of Columbia, South Carolina, designed the 1901 Darlington City Hall. Florence contractor W. J. Wilkins submitted the low bid at $18,650 and broke ground in April 1901. The city hall–opera house was completed in November of the same year, although the steeple was not finished until December. In this c. 1915 photograph, old meets new in front of city hall as two couples pass by, one in a horse-drawn carriage, the other in an automobile. A modern city hall housing the fire department and jail was built in the early 1960s, and the old city hall and Liberty Theater was razed in 1965.

Shoveling snow is not a chore when in Darlington, South Carolina, where it is a rare occurrence. These men work happily to clear the square in front of city hall after the snowfall of February 1914.

This c. 1890 view of Darlington's public square gazes west, across the north side. The photographer was on the top of a new windmill built on the northeast corner of the square at Cashua Street. The smokestack in the left of the skyline belonged to the Darlington Manufacturing Company; in the upper right, the Methodist church (now Trinity United Methodist) is visible, and the Zimmerman and Huggins houses can be seen in the upper left. The *Darlington News* building is in the center, and the newly constructed county jail can be glimpsed in the lower right corner.

This is a c. 1910 view of the south side of Pearl Street, yet unpaved, gazing west from Darlington Square. Telephone service and electricity came to the community some time before the convenience of paved streets. The square was paved in 1920. This photograph was taken by A. T. Hill.

This view of Darlington Square is of Pearl Street's south side from the intersection of McIver Street around 1900. The Enterprise Hotel, soon to become the New Darlington Hotel, is visible on the left. In 1930, a hotel fire consumed much of the square's south side. Rebuilding was one of Darlington's few construction ventures during the years of the Great Depression.

The Darlington Hotel, built in 1884 and operating as the Enterprise Hotel until around 1900, reflects the era of grand old hotels before World War II. Travelers could expect first-class accommodation and service and a formal dining room. Here around 1900, hotel guests on the second-floor balcony relax and enjoy the daily activities on Pearl Street. In 1930, the Darlington Hotel disintegrated in a fiery blaze, killing four people and consuming most of the businesses on the south side of the square.

The Darlington Guards received their charter from the South Carolina Legislature on August 14, 1860, as talk of secession was in the air. On April 7, 1893, the laying of the Darlington Guards Armory cornerstone on the east side of Florence Street (now known as South Main Street) drew merrymakers from all over the county to celebrate the proud event.

This image of a group of Darlington Guards was immediately popular from its creation in 1893, distributed in miniature and in paperweights. Using state-of-the-art processes, the photographer combined at least three different images, beginning with the guards in front of the stage curtains in the armory auditorium layered with a picture of the new armory building.

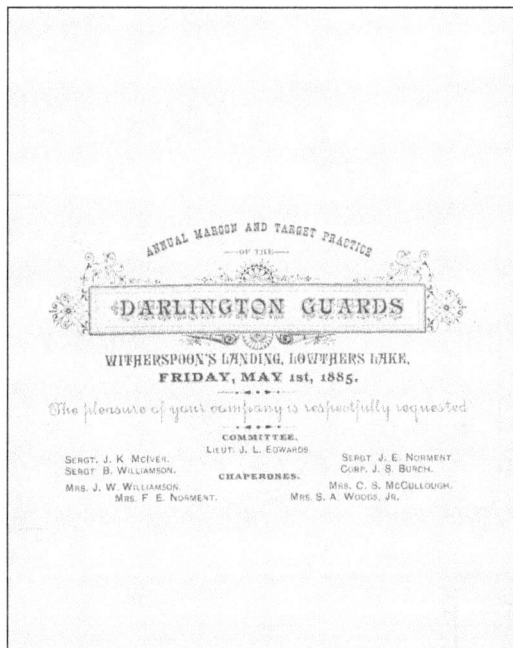

After the construction of the armory on the square in 1893, the Darlington Guards became the center of social activity, organizing lectures and receptions and providing a reading room with popular periodicals of the day. The social event of the year was the much-anticipated maroon encampment, held on Lowther's Lake. "Maroons" included target practice and a picnic, drawing crowds of merrymakers. Here are two formal invitations to the 1885 and 1886 maroons.

The Darlington Guards, pictured in their Spartanburg, South Carolina, encampment on July 4, 1894, are about to receive first prize in a U.S. Army interstate drill. The gentleman kneeling in front of the tent is Charles DuBose; behind him stands Dr. Mack James; and the four men seated in the front are, from left to right, Walter James, David C. Coit, Howard Norment, and Eugene Vaughan. Other guards pictured, although the order is unknown, are Charles McCullough, Louis J. Bristow, Edward Wells, Raymond Harrell, Albert Parrott, Robert James, Tom Rogers, Edwin Cox, P. J. Boatwright, Harold Rast, James Gillespie, Gus Johnson, Louis McCall, Louis Norment, and John Baird.

The Darlington Guards pose for a photographer in 1898 on South Main Street across from the Darlington Guards Armory. In 1878, the Civil War–era militia was reorganized by Col. E. R. McIver. This regiment is prepared to embark for Cuba to fight in the Spanish-American War, the first company in South Carolina to volunteer. Henry "Dad" Brown, the African American drummer for the Darlington Guards, is on the far left with his drum.

Henry "Dad" Brown (1830–1907), an African American brickmason, joined the Confederate States Army in May 1861 as a drummer. Already a veteran of the Mexican–American War, Brown served with the Darlington Grays Company F, 8th South Carolina Infantry, and later joined Company H, 21st South Carolina Infantry, where he served for the remainder of the Civil War. During battle, Brown made a daring capture of a pair of Union drumsticks. He was a member of the Darlington Guards from 1878 until his death in 1907. This is Brown around 1905 at a Memorial Day observance in the courthouse square, with the Confederate monument behind him on the left and the Darlington Guards Armory behind.

John Coleman, a successful tobacco broker, bought the lot on the corner of Pearl Street and the Darlington public square, commissioning a building to replace a "ramshackle wooden store" that existed there, noted a June 23, 1904, *Darlington News* article. Materials and labor in the construction of the Coleman Building, completed in 1902, came to a total of $17,549, a fair price for the three-story brick structure in Second Renaissance Revival style with granite arches and a classic swag-and-wreath motif on the upper section. At right is the Coleman Building as it appeared around 1915, at which time it housed shops on the first floor and offices on the third and fourth floors. The above photograph shows the Coleman Building around 1966, when it housed the Citizens' Bank of Darlington and Willcox Drugstore.

The plight of chain gangs inspired books and movies, but unpaid prison labor was widely exploited in the late 19th century, achieving much public work, such as highway construction, and lining the pockets of many businessmen in the process. Clayton Moody, left, brandishes a pistol before a real 1907 Darlington chain gang. Darlington County supervisor W. S. King designed the cage visible in the background to house prisoners on work detail overnight in other counties. By the 1950s, every state had abolished chain gangs.

The Barringer Hardware Company opened in Darlington in 1927, the epitome of the local, family-owned hardware store that one rarely finds today. Porter's Photography Studio was retained to record Barringer's grand opening. Frank McKeel became a partner in 1942, when the name was changed to Barringer-McKeel Hardware Company. The circular designs on the upper section of the storefront are more than decoration: In this era, iron rods were often run through the interiors of buildings and fastened to exterior walls in an effort to protect them from earthquake damage.

These 1927 grand-opening snapshots of the Barringer Hardware Company's well-stocked interior remind of a time when a visit to the local hardware store was an adventure, and shoppers could purchase wares that ranged from tools, building materials, seeds, gardening supplies, and cookware to a scooter or a red Radio Flyer wagon.

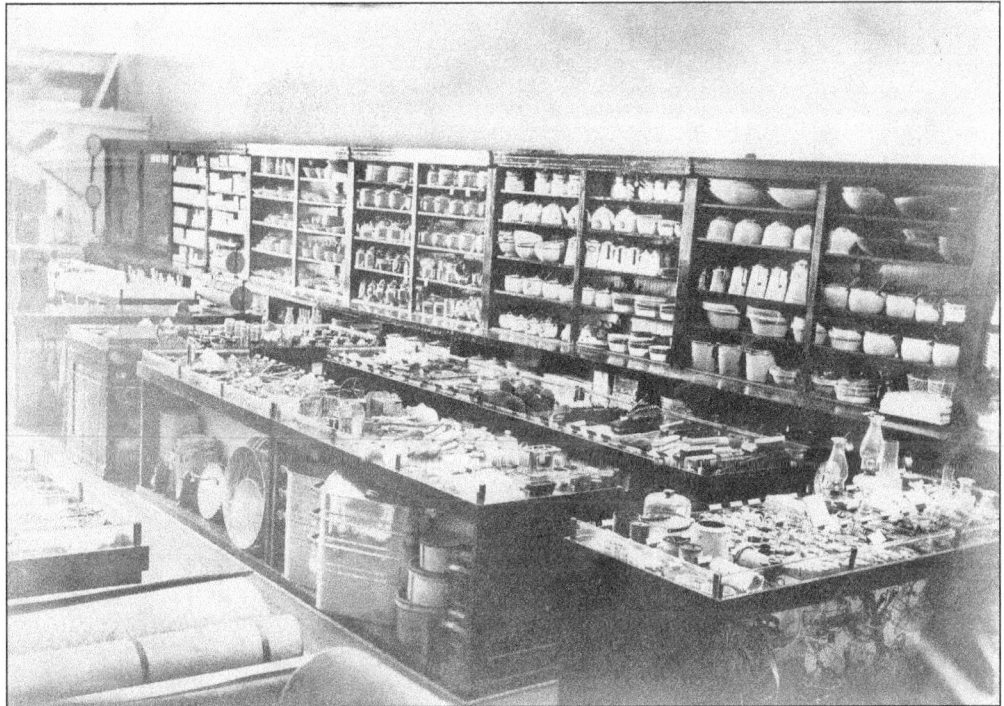

When city policeman W. Oscar Ballard retired from the police force, he turned his energies to a new pastime: the restaurant business. For 16 years, Ballard owned and operated the Deluxe Café on the Darlington public square, offering regulars a fresh seafood special daily. This photograph was taken around 1935.

The Hotel McFall was the "Cleanest Hotel in the State," according to this c. 1925 postcard. Hyman Witcover of Savannah, Georgia, was the architect for the building, first opening in 1915 as the Park Hotel with A. F. Dufft as manager. The hotel accommodated travelers for 60 years under various reincarnations, including the Melrose, the DuBose, and the Park Terrace. In 1968, fire consumed the building, claiming four lives.

HOTEL McFALL.
The Cleanest Hotel in the State
Darlington, S. C.

This image of the Darlington oak shows the tree around 1929, with M. H. Fleming Jr. and M. H. Fleming Sr. standing under its wide-reaching branches.

In the 1940s, the Darlington oak marked the intersection of two streets near the Darlington Armory, headquarters for all local war activity in the county during World War II. Visiting servicemen were often seen strolling around the mighty tree or posing for photographs under its boughs, covering approximately one-fifth of an acre. This photograph was taken in 1949.

The "human fly" scaling the Liberty Theater–city hall in this photograph wears a suit with "1948, DeSoto, Evans Motors" printed on the back, most likely an eye-catching marketing stunt. When the Liberty opened in 1901 as the city hall–opera house, it was immediately a center of attention, and for years, people from all over the county traveled to the Liberty to enjoy popular musical road shows. The opening night performance was the *Village Bride*, presented by the Herald Square Opera Company to a crowded house in evening finery.

W. D. Coggeshall and Company started in business around the beginning of the 20th century, owning a variety of enterprises. Coggeshall's Store has been a fixture on Pearl Street since 1903. The picture on this postcard dates from around 1905. Second from the left is J. "Papa" Hart Coker.

Firefighters rushed to Coggeshall's Store in the wee hours of the morning in January 1995, reaching the burning store in record time. The fire was successfully doused and damages soon repaired.

Darlington's public square welcomed numerous retail establishments over the years. The Belk-Simpson department store was a bustling site as soon as it appeared mid-century, heralding in the age of bobby socks, Burma-Shave, rock and roll, and cars with tailfins and chrome. The store immediately became a part of the community and is shown above shortly after opening in the early 1950s with a parking lot full of eager shoppers. Inside (below), customers browse in the furniture department on the lower floor of Belk-Simpson, looking for the latest in home decor.

Coca-Cola has a long
history, originating
from the recipe of
John Pemberton
and marketed by
Asa Griggs Candler
in the early 20th
century. Coca-Cola
bottling plants
spread rapidly over
the United States in
the 1920s and 1930s.
This c. 1962 image
shows the front
of the Darlington
Coca-Cola bottling
plant on South
Dargan Street
near Pearl Street.
Standing in the
doorway is Cephas
Odom, who delivered
Cokes in the Lamar
and Darlington area
for 19 years.

Electricity, the milking machine,
mechanical refrigeration, and the
wide availability of cars and trucks all
combined to make dairy farming cost-
effective and efficient in the 1930s. John
Blackman of Darlington had a prosperous
dairy farm in the county. This c. 1939
photograph shows his daughter, Lucille
Blackman, leaning against the Blackman's
Dairy delivery truck.

In the days before widespread use of the automobile, livery stables served an important function by offering horses and carriages for hire. This image shows Conder's Livery Stable in 1912, located on Exchange Street in Darlington. The site became the IGA parking lot in 1969. From left to right are an unidentified man, "Shep," owner Henry J. Conder, Charlie Law, and Manly Blackman astride the horse.

Norment's Auto Livery service is advertised on this postcard from around 1915. J. Monroe Spears, a Darlington attorney, successfully raised the funds to replace the shed over Darlington's mineral spring. Spears is the man in the car on the left, seated to the far left. J. E. Norment is behind the car on the far right, standing by the child in the front seat. The center car holds A. F. Dufft, seated next to the driver.

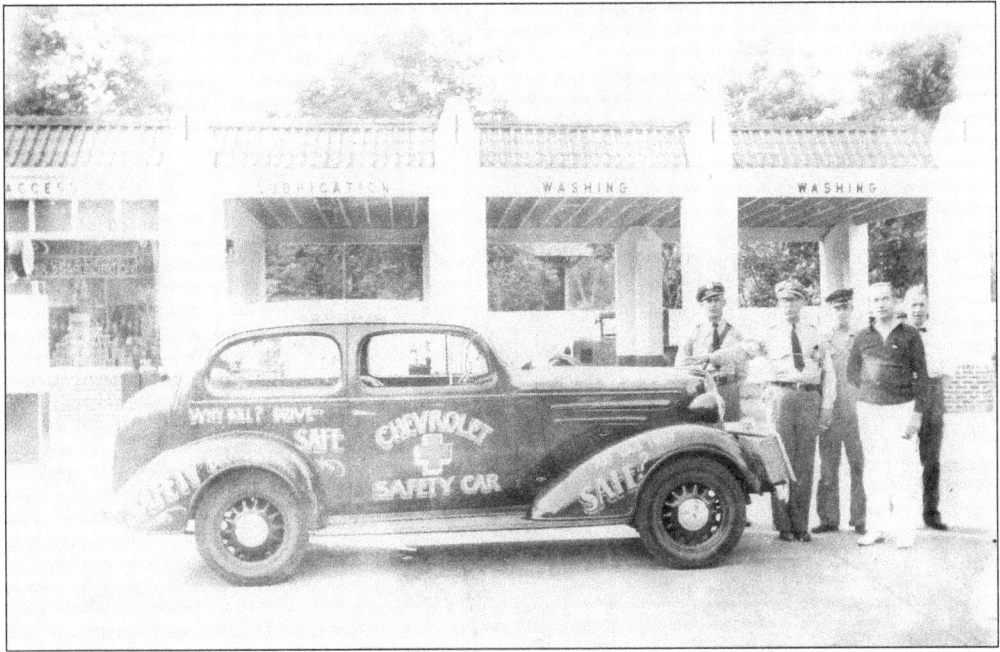

Chevrolet challenged Henry Ford's company by the 1930s with sleek styling and affordable pricing and by capitalizing on its safety features. The Chevrolet Safety Car, pictured here in front of the Darlington Esso station with its driver and a willing audience, is a late-1930s model. Safety cars such as these were marketing tools for the company.

Filling stations became a customary sight on county highways during the 1930s as more and more people owned automobiles. The Darlington filling station and service center in this *c.* 1938 photograph advertises the familiar Esso brand of gasoline. Self-service was unheard of at this time, and the attendant leaning in the doorway could be expected to greet a patron at the car window. Besides filling the gas tank, a customer would be asked, "Check the oil?"

Local writer Elizabeth Boatwright Coker called Black Creek "first and foremost of the woodland amusements of old Darlington." A beloved spot for fishing, swimming, boating, picnicking, and courting, Black Creek spans the centuries in its popularity. Industry along its banks during the 1890s caused concern, and citizens approached a grand jury for assistance in maintaining the creek as a recreation area. By the 1930s, the Black Creek Protective Association formed for that purpose and was granted a state charter in 1941. Above, a group of early-20th-century young ladies in swimming costumes contemplate a dive into the water. The picture at left, also around 1900, shows local women enjoying a refreshing dip.

Good, cool fun never goes out of style. Here bathers from the 1960s experience the same joy splashing and swimming in Black Creek as Darlingtonians did 100 years before. Below, an unidentified group of teenagers enjoy an afternoon of camaraderie, posing on a bank of Black Creek around 1950.

Many Darlington children learned to paddle and do the breaststroke in the tea-colored water of Black Creek. This young swimming party, under the watchful eye of Mother, was photographed around 1912. Maxine Duffet is the second bather from the left.

Galloway's Pool offered relief from steamy South Carolina summers and plenty of fun for Darlingtonians of every age. This photograph taken in June 1938 shows, from left to right, unidentified, J.C. Lofton (boy leaving), Maryjane Weaver, Carroll Nick Merritt (boy with arms extended), Denise Blackman (Holmes), Sarah Lowry (Howle), and Alana McPherson (with her knee on the diving board).

Metro-Goldwyn-Mayer Studios, Inc. (MGM), founded in 1924, dominated the film industry from the silent film era through World War II. When MGM's Leo the Lion trademark went on tour in 1928, the Liberty Theater was one stop. Leo's visit caused a stir in Darlington, and he was greeted in style by town leaders. Here from left to right are police chief S. L. Martin, Liberty's owner G. B. Hendrickson, former mayor E. W. Fountain, and patrolman J. H. Coker.

Olympic gold medal swimmer and actor Johnny Weissmuller gave the world the "Tarzan yell" in the popular MGM *Tarzan the Ape Man* movies, delighting audiences in the late 1920s and 1930s. Here *Tarzan Finds a Son* opens at the Liberty Theater in 1939, starring Weissmuller as Tarzan, Maureen O'Sullivan as Jane, Johnny Sheffield as Boy, and Cheeta the Chimpanzee.

The movie *Wells Fargo*, a western, opened in 1937 starring Joel McCrea and Bob Burns. New movies were anticipated with excitement in the early days of the cinema, especially during the Great Depression, when just a few cents would buy a couple of worry-free hours. This photograph in 1937 was captured before the grand opening of *Wells Fargo* at the popular Liberty Theater in the town square. Employees and movie buffs posing in front of the advertisement are, from left to right, three unidentified, Coke Brown, Mary Phillips Mills, Cleo Belissary, and Shaler Stanley.

Three Little Girls in Blue was a 20th Century Fox musical production filmed in Technicolor in 1946. The Liberty Theater, under the management of George B. Hendrickson, was quick in offering the latest. When talking pictures arrived, Hendrickson did not hesitate to install a Movietone sound system, requiring the operators to tackle the tricky business of synchronizing the sound with the picture. Here to see the show in 1947, from left to right, are devoted movie-goers Robert E. Mills, Mary Phillips Mills, and William "Billy" Hill.

The Darlington County Public Library, pictured here in 1966, was a Carnegie library constructed in 1920, although growing collections and patronage overwhelmed its size in just a few years. Louise McMaster was the first librarian in this building, and the library served patrons 50 hours a week. Bank failures in the late 1920s and early 1930s foiled attempts to expand, but in the mid-1930s, a Works Progress Administration (WPA) construction project doubled the library's size.

Capt. Henry Thompson of the Darlington Guards began the first lending library in Darlington County in the 1880s, first for guard members and their families; later "any gentleman of the community and two ladies of his choice could borrow books" for a fee, said Estellene P. Walker in *So Good and Necessary a World: The Public Library in South Carolina, 1698–1980*. By 1936, the Darlington County Public Library expanded its reach to rural patrons through the purchase of a bookmobile made possible by the Farm Women's Council and the WPA. Three members of the Darlington County library staff are pictured next to the well-stocked bookmobile in 1937.

Edward Hopper's 1942 painting *Nighthawks* captured the unique culture of the 24-hour urban diner. The Southernaire Grill, built in 1948, brought this quintessential 20th-century American experience to Darlington. The art deco streamline architecture made the Southernaire's appearance on Pearl Street thoroughly modern. The grill lasted a mere 20 years, closing in the 1960s.

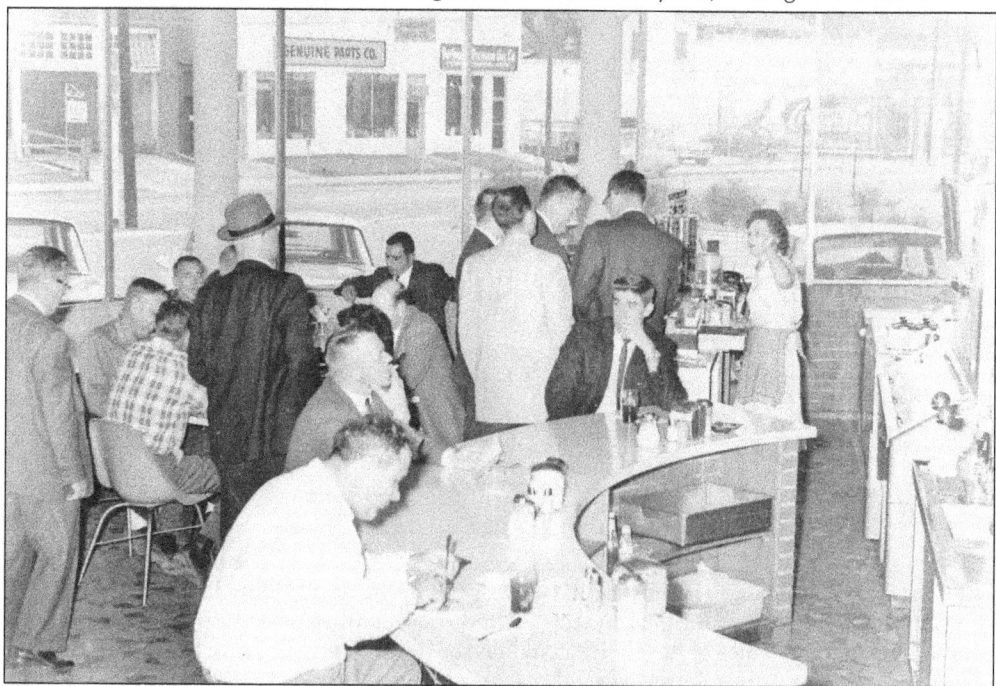

The grill and the curved counter are as much a part of the diner experience as fried eggs, burgers, apple pie, and strong coffee. This is the popular Southernaire Grill during a weekday lunch hour, offering tasty food and service along with a dose of local camaraderie.

The Great Depression, with its accompanying bank failures, deflation, and unemployment, made for hard times in the South Carolina backcountry, as well as the rest of the South. Pres. Franklin D. Roosevelt created the WPA in 1935 to provide jobs and income to the unemployed, especially in rural areas. Projects initiated by the WPA included construction of highways and streets, utilities, city halls, public libraries, and parks. Williamson Park in Darlington was a WPA project. This photograph, showing a section of Swift Creek, was taken later of Williamson Park by the USDA Soil and Conservation Service.

Darlingtonian and retired racer Harold Brasington purchased 70 acres of cotton and peanut fields in 1949, turning them into the first NASCAR super speedway in the country. The Darlington International Raceway held its inaugural race Labor Day, September 4, 1950, hosting 75 racers, with an estimated 30,000 people in attendance. Johnny Mantz of Long Beach, California, drove his 1950 Plymouth coupe over the finish line first, winning an $11,500 prize. This photograph shows curious onlookers admiring the raceway as it nears completion in 1949.

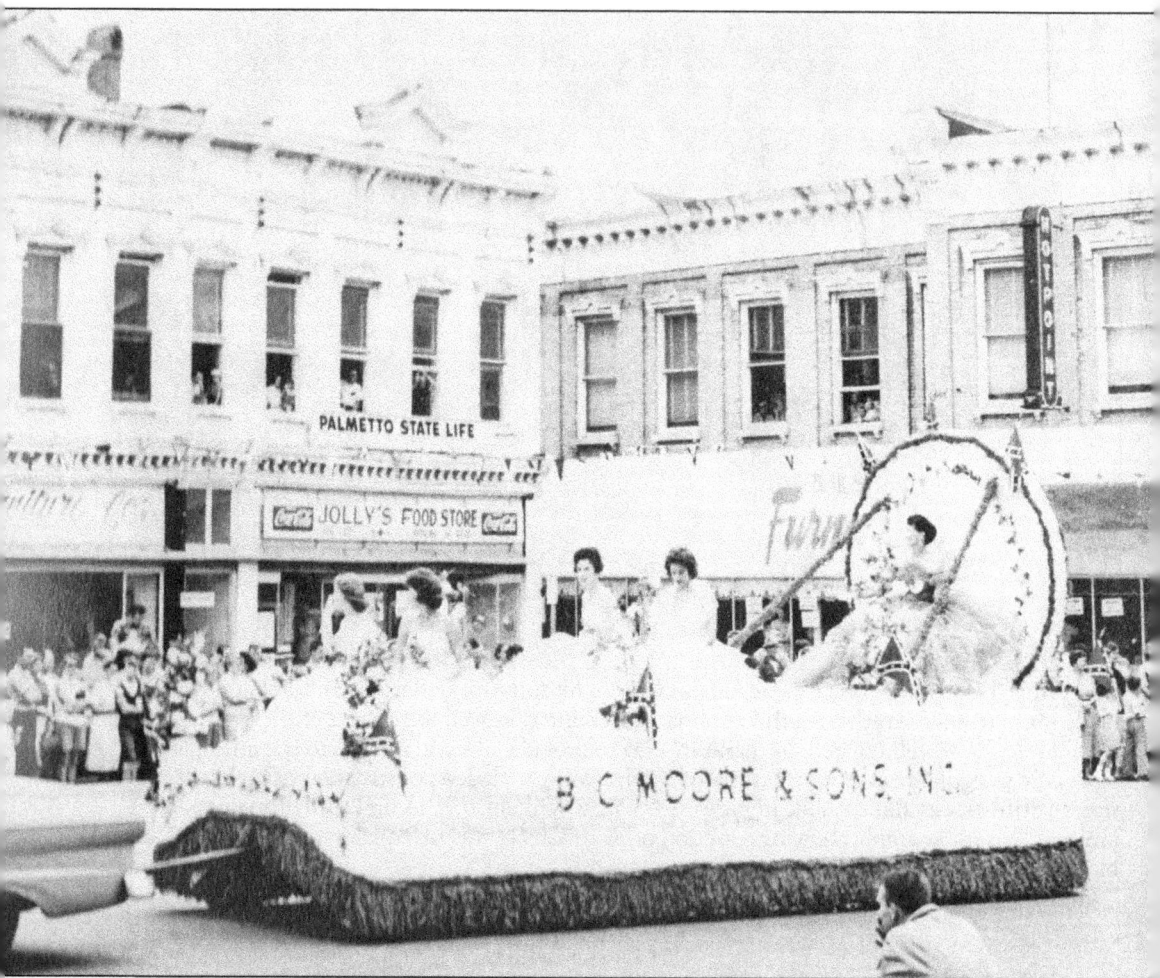

Accompanying the annual Labor Day race at the Darlington International Raceway was the popular Southern 500 parade. The festivities meant lots of visitors and revenue for Darlington business owners, as thousands of people poured into town. This decorative B. C. Moore and Sons, Inc., parade float makes its way through the Darlington square, past the enthusiastic crowd on the street and in the windows above, around 1955. Southern 500 Queen Caroline Sansbury (Humphries) waves a white-gloved hand to admirers from her seat at the rear.

Two

HARTSVILLE

In 1817, Thomas Edwards Hart (1794–1842) and his wife, Hannah Lide, purchased 8,000 acres of pristine wooded land on Black Creek. In 1838, after petitioning the general assembly for a public road connecting Darlington District with the Pee Dee River and Society Hill, Hart opened a general store and served as postmaster of the Hartsville Post Office.

Farming in the area was lucrative, and when cotton prices soared in 1835, many planters purchased land and slaves on credit. However, a country-wide economic depression combined with a poor cotton crop in 1837 buffeted area cotton merchants and business owners, resulting in heavy financial loss and debt.

Personal and financial destitution in the aftermath of the Civil War did not dampen the spirit of Maj. James Lide Coker (1837–1918). Coker embarked on his first commercial venture in 1865, and the J. L. Coker and Company mercantile opened in Thomas Hart's old store. Over the next decades, reliable rail service developed, and by the 1890s, industry thrived in Hartsville. Major Coker and his son, James L. Coker, formed the Carolina Fibre Company, a paper mill, and the Southern Novelty Company, which operates today as Sonoco Products Company.

Answering to the town's prosperity, the Bank of Hartsville opened in 1903. From 1900 to 1920, Hartsville gained a paper mill, cottonseed oil mill, wood manufacturing company, marble works, silver company, and fertilizer manufacturer. Still, agriculture remained the mainstay of the community; the tobacco market flourished, and Hartsville's market for long-staple cotton was one of the largest in the South. Population tripled during this time, and churches and schools were established to accommodate the growing community.

WPA projects in the 1930s established an armory, a library, a civic center, an airport, and paved roads. In mid-century, residential neighborhoods cropped up outside the city proper, fueled by the expansion of roads and the popularity of the automobile. In 1958, Hartsville acquired a steam electric generating plant on Black Creek, later converted into a nuclear power plant by the Carolina Light and Power Company. Hartsville today combines industry, agriculture, and education with a family-friendly atmosphere.

Cotton wagons make their way down Carolina Avenue toward the cotton yard of the Coker Cotton Company around 1915. The company, founded by David R. Coker (1870–1938), stood at the intersection of Carolina Avenue and Fifth Street, just behind the J. L. Coker and Company store. Carroll Chase captured this image when cotton was still the crop of choice in Darlington County, bringing the best return for the investment.

These farmers are selling cotton at the Coker Cotton Company around 1920. Coker's Pedigreed Seed Catalog, first published in 1914, offered advice on seed breeding and better farming techniques in general. Gabe Stokes (1863–1946) is the third from the left, waiting in line to have the quality of the crop assessed. W. H. Sory (1886–1967) is the cotton buyer standing at the counter to the right, inspecting samples.

J. L. Coker and Company handled payroll and banking functions for the Hartsville community until 1903, when the Hartsville Bank began operation with a capital stock of $50,000. J. L. Coker was president, A. M. McNair was vice president, and L. Vaughan was cashier. This photograph from a postcard shows the bank in 1909.

Maj. James Lide Coker, Civil War veteran and entrepreneur, was instrumental in establishing numerous business ventures in Hartsville and established the Welsh Neck High School, which later became Coker College. Here Charles Westfield Coker, grandson of Major Coker and later executive vice president of Sonoco Products Company, takes his brand-new buggy for a spin through Hartsville in 1898.

This is the home of Maj. James Lide Coker photographed around 1909. Major Coker married Susan Armstrong Stout in 1860, and they had 10 children: James Jr., Francis, David, William, Thomas, Charles, Margaret, Hannah, Jennie, and Susan. The residence burned to the ground in 1922.

Pictured here are the surviving members of Hartsville Military Company E, Confederate States Army, in a c. 1910 reunion at the home of Maj. James Lide Coker.

The Norwood family settled in Darlington County in its early years, engaging in turpentine production, and continued through the years as prominent businessmen and bankers in the community. This is W. L. Norwood, right, driving past Hartsville's Crescent Café with a friend around 1907.

Hartsville's Arcade Hotel, designed by J. Maner Lawton, opened in 1913 at 204 North Fifth Street, signaling the development of Hartsville as a focal point for commerce and industry in the region. This photograph shows the hotel in 1914. A three-story brick building with an entrance portico, the Arcade boasted an elegant lobby, dining room, barbershop, and 42 guest rooms. The hotel was listed in the National Register of Historic Places in 1986.

This is a c. 1918 photograph of the Edward E. Carnes House, which stood on the fashionable southwest corner of East Carolina Avenue and Second Street. Note the style of the wraparound porch and the grape arbor, a common fixture in yards of the South. Sweet muscadine grapes are naturally disease and pest resistant, particularly enjoying the humidity and sandy soil of South Carolina. The hardy grape proved excellent in jams and jellies and just right for canning. Muscadine wine was one of the most popular drinks in the United States before Prohibition. The people in front of the house are unidentified.

The Temple Theater was built in the early 1900s as an auditorium and meeting place, but by the 1920s, a movie screen was added. Wilmot Berry recalled that teenage boys attending a show liked to sit in the balcony, eating peanuts and throwing them at the occasional rat that inhabited the building. By the early 1930s, the theater had closed, and a vegetable market conducted business inside. This image shows the theater toward the end of its existence. In total disrepair, the Temple was torn down, to be replaced by the new Center Theater in 1935, a WPA initiative.

The hearse pictured here belonged to the Pennington Funeral Home on West Carolina Avenue, owned by Carol Melvin Pennington Sr. The funeral parlor opened in 1915, the same year the hearse was manufactured for a horse-drawn vehicle. In the 1920s, the hearse was placed on a Ford Model T truck, as it appears in this photograph. The Brown brothers, Heyward, Loraine, and Claude, owned a monument works in Hartsville and merged with the Pennington Funeral Home in 1939.

Here Carolina Avenue enjoys celebration and relief over the armistice signed between the Allies and Germany on the Western Front in a railway carriage November 11, 1918, ending World War I. This photograph shows Hartsville's Armistice celebration in November 1918. Edward E. Carnes Jr. poses for the camera as a flag is raised in the intersection of Carolina Avenue and Fifth Street. H. Leland Law stands on the right.

Snow does not come often to South Carolina, so when it does it causes much excitement. This undated photograph, taken around 1910, captures the beauty of an unexpected snowfall on West Home Avenue. A lone motorist braves the road.

This photograph shows the Edward E. Carnes house at the corner of East Carolina Avenue and Second Street after a rare snowfall in 1920. Edward E. Carnes Jr. is pictured experiencing the snow, with Martha Carnes behind.

44

MAY 25, 1946

Children's birthday parties in the 1940s were not the extravagant affairs of recent years but were anticipated eagerly and were just as much fun. And some things remain the same: This group of young celebrants in 1946 sports party hats and blows noisemakers for the camera before enjoying cake and ice cream. Mary Mozingo donated the photograph to the Darlington County Historical Commission archives.

The Hartsville Fire Department shows off its brand-new, state-of-the-art fire engine in front of the firehouse around 1915. The proud firefighters posing for the photograph are fire chief D. B. Shaw (left) and Julian S. Moore.

Fire chief D. B. Shaw (left) and firefighter W. D. Arthur (right) of the Hartsville Fire Department pose for the camera in front of the Carolina Power and Light Company building around 1920. On the back of the truck, an honorary fire dog proudly sits for the picture.

These are the members of Hartsville's police force in the late 1930s, pictured in front of police headquarters. From left to right are Joseph Bunch, Clyde Sullivan, John Henry Williams, V. C. Elmore, ? Horne, and two unidentified policemen.

Municipal airports began appearing in the United States in the mid- to late 1920s. The Hartsville Municipal Airport opened in the early 1930s with a runway of 5,000 feet and an elevation of 364 feet. This is the main entrance to the Hartsville Municipal Airport around 1932.

Segars' Bathing Resort at Segars' Mill, four miles west of Hartsville on Highway 35, was chartered in 1920 by H. K. Segars, E. H. Segars, and J. C. Hungerpiller as part of an amusement park. A c. 1940 poster urges bathers to "Ride the Ropes at Segars' Bathing Resort," offering an in-pool merry-go-round, spring creek water on a sandy bottom, glowing wells, a pavilion, boating and fishing on the lake, and camping and picnic grounds. The above 1937 image shows bathers frolicking beneath the carousel and the ropes. The first-floor ticket office and women's bathhouse are visible on the left. The image at left, also in the late 1930s, captures one of the many awe-inspiring dives executed over the years in the cool water of Beaver Dam Creek at Segars' Bathing Resort.

After 1910, Hartsville slipped into an economic depression, echoing conditions in the rest of the state. The WPA, established in the 1930s during Franklin D. Roosevelt's administration, provided jobs to the many South Carolinians in need of employment. Lawton Park was one of the many projects completed through the program in Hartsville. This undated photograph shows the Lawton Park Pavilion, most likely in the late 1930s. Lucille Boswell Neely donated this image to the archives, noting on the back that "there was a nice playground" in Lawton Park.

This postcard—mailed in 1936 from a student at Columbia College in Columbia, South Carolina, to Mittie Read Fields in Lydia—shows a scene from Kalmia Gardens, now part of the Coker College campus. In the early 1930s, May Roper Coker transformed a neglected dump site into a 30-acre botanical garden complete with a pond and trails and featuring native plants such as *Kalmia latifolia*, a species of mountain laurel that presents clusters of star-shaped flowers in the early summer months ranging in color from red to pink to white.

This aerial image of Hartsville, facing the southeast, was captured around 1938. Not long before, the parallel parking visible on Carolina Avenue replaced center-street parking. A new city hall and fire station replaced Coker's Gin on Carolina Avenue in 1950.

This is a picturesque view of Fifth Street around 1940. The automobile was clearly here to stay, as busy shoppers stock up on supplies at B. C. Moore and Sons department store (still located at 827 South Fifth Street), Center Sports, and Corner Drugs, perhaps taking time for lunch and coffee at the Manhattan Coffee Shop. Frigidaire, popular since its formation in 1918, made its presence known among the stores lining the avenue.

This is a late-1960s view of Carolina Avenue at the intersection of Fifth Street showing the Berry Theater in the background to the right. First there was the Temple Theater, facing Fifth Street where Centennial Park is now. Then the Center Theater, built with WPA labor in 1935, served Hartsville as a venue for performing arts and a movie theater during World War II through the 1950s. By 1965, the Center Theater had fallen into disrepair, and for $200,000, it was restored and renamed the Berry.

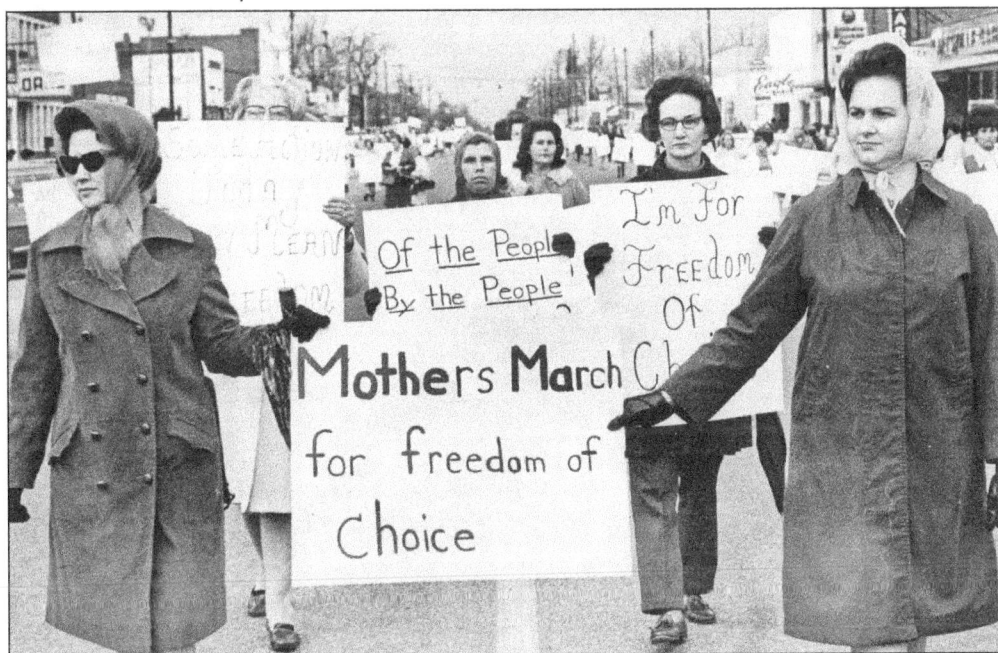

The United States was bitterly divided on a number of issues throughout the 1960s. The age of *The Feminine Mystique* brought the women's liberation movement, and Betty Friedan founded the National Organization of Women (NOW) in 1966. Women faced a number of difficult concerns, from working outside of the home to developing political skills. In this news photograph taken in February 1970, several women make a bold political statement during a peaceful protest on Carolina Avenue.

Carolina Avenue's appearance changed over time but remained just as lovely. This is East Carolina Avenue in October 1973, now lined with more cars and shaded by mature oak trees.

Hartsville continues to expand in the new millennium. Here the historic meets the modern as ground is broken in 2000 for a Wal-Mart Supercenter at Hartsville Crossing Boulevard on 1150 South Fourth Street. City leaders insisted that Wal-Mart not use its traditional colors, instead requiring the corporation to conform to the town's own aesthetic specifications.

Three

RUSTIC COMMUNITIES

Society Hill is the oldest town in Darlington County. The community began as Long Bluff in the 1750s on the west bank of the Pee Dee River, with a boat landing and trading post. The first courthouse and jail were erected in 1769, and a store, tavern, and homes soon materialized. Emotions and notions of freedom ran high in Long Bluff in the years preceding the Revolutionary War: In 1774, taxes levied by the British Parliament incited local men to declare their right to obey only laws passed by elected officials of the district. After the American Revolution, St. David's Academy was built on a hill, prompting the community to become known as "Society's Hill."

Lamar is the youngest town in Darlington County, developing from a trading post in the 1850s at a crossroad on Capt. George Mims's plantation. The intersection soon attracted a general store, school, and the doctor's office of E. J. Mims. First known as Lisbon, South Carolina, the new Lamar Post Office reopened in 1886, named after Sen. Lucius Quintus Cincinnatus Lamar of Mississippi.

Turpentine and timber industries first defined Lamar, and the partnership of Mims and Reynolds erected the first turpentine still. The Charleston, Sumter, and Northern Railroad made Lamar a connection between Darlington and Sumter, and as a result population increased. During the Great Depression of the 1930s, the town went bankrupt, but by the 1950s, Lamar rebounded as a profitable tobacco market. Federal desegregation and the civil rights movement unfolded painfully, and in the 1970s, racial violence plunged the little community into the national news. Lamar rallied, and a new town hall, a police station, and a popular spring festival, the Egg Scramble, now exist to greet visitors.

Other communities, including Antioch Township, Auburn, Clyde, Dovesville, Indian Branch, Jasper, Lumber, Lydia, Oates, and Palmetto Township, each lend unique personalities and stories to the county's historical narrative.

Evan's Mill Pond, in Society Hill, built before the American Revolution, was once known as Dewitt's Mill after its owner, Capt. William Dewitt. Samuel Desurrency was first granted the land in 1744, and it is likely that he built the small lake. This image of a group of friends enjoying the afternoon fishing at the old millpond dates from 1906.

The Revolutionary War left many scars in the Darlington District, as Whigs and Tories fought one another bitterly. The death of Whig sympathizer Col. Abel Kolb, whose father was an original settler of the Welsh tract, was particularly poignant. After successfully rousting a group of Tories on the Pee Dee in 1781, Colonel Kolb was ambushed in his home by a vengeful group of Tories, then killed in the act of surrendering his sword. The Old Welsh Neck Church Cemetery, now part of Marlboro County, contains a monument later erected by the Daughters of the American Revolution. The man pictured is Abner Turner, who has just restored the foundation of the monument around 1930.

The earliest "social" lending library in the backcountry region was the Society Hill Library, founded in 1822. The St. David's Society originated the Society Hill Library Society, selecting books consisting of "Biography, History, Travel, Science, also fiction by standard authors, Dickens, Scott, Thackery and others," according to Sue S. Wilson in *Darlingtoniana*. The building was renovated in 1971 and still remains part of the Darlington County Library System, although it is not in the original location. Librarian Sue Wilson (1873–1974) served Society Hill for many years, as well loved by patrons as was the library.

Once known as the McIntosh house and built between 1795 and 1810, when this image was captured around 1900, the home belonged to Rev. J. W. Burn. The Burn family was one of the earliest families in the Society Hill community, and Rev. J. W. Burn was the first pastor of the First Baptist Church in Hartsville in the last quarter of the 19th century, coming into possession of this house around 1850. Pictured on the front steps are members of both sides of the family. From left to right are (first row) Bryan Burn, Sadie Burn, Harold Heustess, Beulah Womack, and Bernard Womack; (second row) Florence Burn, Mrs. Jim Heustess, Susan B. Womack, Sarah King, Elizabeth A. Crowell, Mrs. H. C. Burn, and Hannah Burn; (third row) H. C. Burn, Jim Heustess, H. A. Womack, Frank Burn, Henry B. Burn, and Edward Burn. Standing to the side on the right are cook Martha Hopkins and her daughter, Bertha, behind here. The image at left is a print of a *c.* 1879 daguerreotype showing Henry C. Burn standing in front of his carpentry shop.

These undated portraits, probably from the early 1860s, are of Henry C. Burn's wife, Jane A. McIntosh Burns, right, and Henry Cassels Burn, below, of Kershaw's Brigade, an elite South Carolina company in Gen. Robert E. Lee's army during the Civil War. Henry C. Burn later became a superintendent of education in the state and served in the House of Representatives from 1890 to 1892.

Lined with oak trees, this is a view down Main Street in Society Hill around 1900 near the old post office. T. A. Gandy Sr. stands on the right. As the century moved on, the post office became the telephone exchange, and Main Street was crisscrossed with telephone wires. The street was paved in the late 1930s as part of a statewide South Carolina Department of Transportation highway project.

Young Glenn Carrigan (left) and Fred Winters of Society Hill take Dr. W. A. Carrigan's Ford touring car for a spin in the summer of 1911. This is an early Model T, made on Henry Ford's Detroit assembly line and first marketed in 1908. The popular touring car model was manufactured until 1926, when more efficient designs overtook the Model T.

Edward W. Laney Jr., a Society Hill deputy sheriff, poses for the camera on Main Street around 1939. Coker and Rogers Store, an enduring landmark in Society Hill for almost 160 years, appears in the background. The Coca-Cola sign invites visitors to stop in for an ice-cold fountain beverage on a hot South Carolina day, perhaps accompanied by a Moon Pie. Laney later became chief of police and a magistrate.

S. W. Fields (1892–1968) perches atop his car, parked in front of his Society Hill house, around 1945. Fields was a magistrate for Society Hill.

The Dargan family of Back Swamp, South Carolina, is captured here in this print from a platinotype made in 1897 on the occasion of a family reunion. From left to right are (first row) Eliza Hart Dargan, Joseph F. Dargan, Sarah Dubose Dargan (Mrs. W. E. Dargan II), and W. E. Dargan II; (second row) Edna Dargan, Henry Flinn Dargan, Karl Dargan, Benton Dargan, W. E. Dargan III, Walter Dargan, and Ida Louise Dargan.

Three generations of the Windham family pose for the camera in front of the old homestead at Windham's Crossroads around 1902. From left to right are Leon Roland Windham, Mrs. Roland Windham, John Windham, Harold Windham, Marie Windham, Emmaline Stokes Windham, Sarah Windham (sister of Leon Roland), and farmhand Ira Dorrity on horse Ben.

Bridges are a necessary part of living near the Pee Dee and play a large role in the river's history. Floods could be expected, and while welcome freshets at the right time of year provided fertile sediment for nearby soil, major flooding could entirely wash out a bridge, effectively halting activities. Here is the Pee Dee River Bridge in 1908 after flood damage.

This is a view approaching the entrance to the old Pee Dee River Bridge in Society Hill in 1909, after it was abandoned because of flood damage. The Society Hill Bridge Board was created in the early 1920s to look into constructing a new bridge. By 1925, the Hampton Construction Company of Washington, D.C., began building a new steel bridge for an estimated $64,000. A toll was enacted to pay costs but was lifted in 1930 when the South Carolina Department of Transportation stepped in. In 1947, yet another bridge was built over the Pee Dee at the Society Hill site, and this bridge was moved and reconstructed just below Kolb's Ferry.

Railroads began to come through Darlington County in the 1850s, although many people were ambivalent about this new form of travel. No one desired the tracks to come too close to town. The Atlantic Coast Line Railroad was one of the first in the region, taking over the Hartsville Railroad Company in the early 1890s to connect several towns in the county. This *c.* 1912 image shows the Society Hill water tower, situated on the tracks near the Cedar Creek trestle to serve the railroad.

Rail travelers await their train at the busy Society Hill depot of the Cheraw and Darlington Railroad around 1910. The horse and buggy in the foreground highlights the intersection of two forms of travel, one new and one old. It took the affordable automobile to finally replace the horse-drawn carriage.

This is the busy Atlantic Coast Line Railroad depot at Lumber, South Carolina, around 1910, when the village was at its population of almost 1,000 people. The depot served both passengers and freight for the Bridgers-McKeithan Lumber Company, and Western Union had a telegraph office situated inside.

The Cheraw and Darlington Railroad (C&D), directed by Maj. B. D. Townsend, came through Darlington Village in 1856. Union troops passing through Darlington in March 1865 burned the depot and its surrounding platforms and trestles, but Darlington itself suffered little damage. Standing in front of the rebuilt C&D Railroad Depot in 1896 are Capt. A. F. Edwards II (right), Mrs. J. B. Edwards holding infant J. B. Edwards, and Hannah Edwards. The C&D Railroad Depot was torn down a final time during World War II.

The Atlantic Coast Line Railroad (ACL) was one of the earliest rail lines to come through Darlington County, connecting several small towns. Here is one of the ACL depots around 1950, alerting riders that they had reached Lamar.

Like many historic buildings, the Lamar ACL depot was reinvented over time, serving numerous purposes over the years. Around 1959, the structure was the property of Harold Andrews and served as a hardware and lumber store known as Andrews and Sons. By the time this photograph was taken by Howard Waddell in 1985, the depot was known as Bow Building Company Supply. The old ACL depot went out in a blaze of glory: on May 22, 2007, Darlington County Fire Station 12, Lamar 15, Lake Swamp, and Lydia received a 5:00 a.m. call, and a total of 50 firefighters responded as the warehouse was consumed by flames. The cause of the fire was traced to burning debris on an adjacent property.

Henry Ford introduced the Model T in 1908, when the automobile was hardly an ordinary machine. The pride captured in this 1909 photograph is evident, as these Ford touring cars, sometimes called the Tin Lizzie or the Flivver, take a spin through Lumber. Passengers in the car at left are W. D. McIver (left), Mrs. W. D. McIver, and Key Lampley. The second car holds, from left to right, O. V. King, Thelma King, Vivien King, and Mrs. O. V. King.

Shannon's roadway Esso station at the intersection of U.S. 15 and U.S. 52 capitalized on President Eisenhower's interstate highway initiative, Americans' growing fondness for the automobile, and a delectable Southern treat: the pecan. The two state roads intersect at Society Hill. This postcard was produced around 1955.

Stafford's Grocery had been in business for more than two decades when this photograph was taken in 1961. The fork in the road was the intersection of U.S. 401 and U.S. 601. Motorists traveling right headed toward Hartsville, and those traveling left soon reached Darlington. In the late 1970s, the highway names changed to U.S. 52 and U.S. 15, respectively.

Essential items as well as treats could be purchased at the Stokes Grocery Store in Lamar, founded by Burdine S. Stokes in 1899 and located adjacent to the old Watson building. This photograph shows the interior of the well-stocked grocery around 1920. Pictured by the counter to the left are B. S. Stokes (left) and his son, Haywood Stokes.

The McSween Mercantile Company was founded in Timmonsville, South Carolina, around 1877 by John McSween, a native of Scotland. This c. 1920 photograph shows the Lamar branch of the company, built in 1910. McSween Mercantile remained Lamar's largest department store for many decades. The store sold everything from flour and other household staples, clothing, and shoes to automobile tires.

The Bank of Lamar, chartered in 1904 with an operating capital of $10,000, failed just seven years later in 1911. This image is on a postcard dated 1906, sent from Florence, South Carolina, to Cora and S. Dubose, students at Columbia College in Columbia, South Carolina. Dr. James A. Cole was the bank president, and the man pictured in the doorway may be O. B. Jordan of Lamar, the institution's first cashier.

Banks are an essential element in any town's economy, expressing security and prosperity. Here R. Bethea Scarborough, left, stands near Frank Carl Huff in the teller's window of the People's Bank in Lamar around 1919.

A group of unidentified sales clerks and shoppers pose for the camera in this early Lamar store, probably a grocery and bakery shop, around 1915. Notice the rolling cart bearing the National Biscuit Company name that the young man to the right is leaning upon. The National Biscuit Company manufactured the popular Uneeda brand of mass-produced cookies and crackers. We know the company today as Nabisco.

John F. Sparrow (1875–1938), rural mail carrier, delivers the mail by horse-drawn wagon in the Indian Branch community around 1915. Rural mail carriers, chosen by the local postmaster, sold stamps, envelopes, and postcards to customers in addition to delivering and picking up mail. Braving rain, hail, sleet, and cold, mail carriers knew everyone on their routes and could expect to stop for a chat or sometimes be invited in for a slice of cake or freshly baked cookies.

Lamar chief of police Ira Fields, on the far right, poses around 1924 with his family in front of his house.

In February 1954, the town of Lamar turned out to meet a red, three-ton fire engine that blazed into town with lights flashing and siren blaring. The engine, purchased during the term of Mayor Daily Harris, replaced the old hose cart, seen in the background to the right. Here town leaders pose proudly with the new addition. From left to right are E. H. Segars Sr., Dr. T. J. Boykin, Daily Harris, Dallas Mackie, Bob Coker, and Gary Parnell (fire chief and chief of police).

Lamar Community Fire Department, all volunteer, was called into action soon after the new fire engine drove into town, when a house fire required their services. The firefighters in this 1954 photograph are unidentified, but the fire department roster for that year listed Lamar citizens Willie Prosser, Bill Thomas, Dewey King, Clarence Fields, Grier Harris, John William Lane, Willard Carter, James Wright, Harry Rowell, and J. B. Lane.

The Finer Carolina Project was an initiative undertaken by the state in the 1950s to modernize and improve public areas. Lamar chose five projects for their Finer Carolina program. The first and most exciting was turning the old ACL bed into an airplane landing strip. This photograph was taken in 1950 as three people indicate the clearing where the new airstrip would be installed.

The South Carolina Breakfast Club, a group of pilots and their family members who get together twice a month for breakfast at different airports in the state, began meeting in 1938 and are still active today. Here in 1954, chief of police Gary Parnell waits by the landing strip to greet one of the pilots arriving for a meeting in Lamar. Mayor Daily Harris is credited with making numerous civic improvements in Lamar in the early 1950s, and the Lamar airport was one such project. In 1954, Lamar residents Harold Segars and Marvin White owned the only two home-based airplanes.

Although the location of this police station in Lamar, built in 1963, was chosen for its excellent view of town in all four directions, it remained in use for less than 20 years. In the early 1980s, the Lamar Police Department moved into a state-of-the-art city hall, jail, and fire department complex. Here in 1964 are, from left to right, Gary Parnell, Baxter Windham, Wayne King, R. Pike Reynolds, F. C. Humphries, G. Greer Harris, Mayor Thomas W. Hill, and Barney E. Hardin.

Dr. Theo J. Boykin, from the Newman Swamp area of Darlington County, served the town of Lamar as mayor for 31 years. Boykin attended Birmingham and Memphis Medical Colleges, receiving his degree from the University of Nashville in 1911. His brother, Gary Boykin, also a medical doctor, owned the Boykin Hotel on Lamar's Main Street early in the 20th century. This c. 1960 photograph shows then-mayor Greer Harris presenting a plaque to Dr. T. J. Boykin commemorating years of loyal service. From left to right are Kitty Harris, Greer Harris, Dr. Theo J. Boykin, and Mrs. T. J. Boykin.

Four

AGRICULTURE, INDUSTRY, AND ENTREPRENEURSHIP

Lowcountry planters in the Colonial years produced indigo and rice. Devastation accompanying the American Revolution, combined with increased international competition, marked the end of coastal agricultural prosperity. The cultivation of short-staple cotton, initially difficult and labor-intensive to process, was made efficient through Eli Whitney's cotton gin, and the backcountry capitalized on the trend. By 1820, cotton was the wave of South Carolina's future, and backcountry yeoman farmers were well prepared to propagate the crop.

Cotton mills provided employment, but paychecks were meager. Mill villages surrounded factories, offering employees low-cost housing but molding every aspect of tenants' lives. Child labor persisted in Southern textile mills into the 20th century.

Tobacco production in Darlington County began in the 1880s as a small-scale cash crop. Local planters B. F. Smoot and E. E. McGill built the Darlington Tobacco Warehouse, one of the first successful tobacco warehouses in the region. In 1920, both tobacco and cotton prices collapsed due to overproduction, loss of international markets, and the boll weevil. After World War I, tobacco overtook cotton production in the Pee Dee region, and it continues as the number one crop today.

Railroads came to Darlington County in the 1850s. The Wilmington and Manchester line was the first, traversing the county from east to west and passing Darlington Court House within 10 miles. The Cheraw and Darlington rail line was built soon after, connecting the Wilmington and Manchester to the town of Cheraw. By the 1880s, the Timmonsville and Lydia provided travelers an efficient way to reach the town of Oates, where William J. Oates (1826–1897) owned a general store and post office.

In the 1920s, after the Great War, South Carolina faced difficult times. Crop failures and bank failures contributed to a cash flow problem long before the stock market crashed in 1929. The WPA benefited Darlington County, providing jobs and public works. The Darlington Racetrack in 1950 reshaped county demographics and produced a wave of tourism.

A leitmotif through Darlington County history is the resourcefulness of her citizens in seizing on possibilities. Creativity and entrepreneurship characterize Darlingtonians' ability to adapt and survive.

These cotton-pickers on the Moore farm in Ashland, South Carolina, pause for a photograph around 1900. The man second from the left is Etson King. While many Southerners amassed fortunes in the cotton market, many more people, black and white, endured the labor-intensive process of cotton cultivation. Until World War II, most tasks associated with cotton production—plowing, cultivating, and harvesting—were completed through manual labor, and sharecropping trapped farmers, both tenants and owners, in a cycle of poverty.

In keeping with Gilded Age America's industrial trend, Society Hill added a brick production yard, first chartered as A. C. Spain and Company in 1890. Later the company was acquired by Bright Williamson and John Blackman, and the name changed to the Darlington Brick Company. Bricks were produced by the plant until the 1950s. This image shows workers on the production line around 1914.

The Darlington Manufacturing Company, a cotton mill established in 1884, was an early example of the industry that would burgeon in the county by the 1890s. This is the engine room of the company around 1895, with the maintenance crew of the Harris Corliss 350-horsepower steam engine. These powerful machines were used in textile and steel mills, waterworks, or any industry requiring large amounts of power.

The Charleston, Sumter, and Northern Railroad, connecting Darlington to Bennettsville in 1890, made the Bridgers-McKeithan Lumber Company possible. Around 1900, D. T. McKeithan set up a sawmill operation in Lumber on the Pee Dee River, adjacent to the railroad. Soon a company village grew around the sawmill, with workers' houses, a post office, school, commissary, church, and a three-story hotel, visible in this c. 1905 image of the Bridgers-McKeithan Lumber Company yard.

This is the Darlington Ginning, Milling, and Fertilizer Company around 1898, with manager T. C. Shores standing on the porch, second from left. The company was chartered in 1888.

The Hartsville Oil Mill, opening in 1900 as a subsidiary of J. L. Coker and Company, extracted the oil from cottonseed to create a number of products, one a high-protein animal feed. In this photograph, Ransom S. Galloway stands in front of the wagon wheel before a load of cotton brought into the mill around 1912. The Hartsville Oil Mill continues in operation today, located in Darlington.

This is the original building of Maj. James Lide Coker's Southern Novelty Company, pictured around 1909. Established in 1899, the company eventually became Sonoco and continues to provide packaging products. The old building, bearing many additions, lasted well into the 1970s.

John E. Sumner and Sons store operated for many years, known as John E. Sumner when the company organized in the 1890s and later adding the sons as partners. In 1970, Sumner and Sons sold to Mr. and Mrs. R. D. King, and King Mercantile operated for 10 years. The building was vacant when it caught fire and burned to the ground in the 1980s. This photograph of the store was taken around 1949.

Milliner and businesswoman Gillie Mims operated a hat shop in Lamar around 1900 in the building that later became the Cash Grocery Store, owned and operated by I. W. Reynolds. Around 1930, Reynolds's son, J. Perry Reynolds, began his own mercantile business in a building just next door. One of the customary services offered by mercantile establishments was delivery. Pictured here in front of J. P. Reynolds's eye-catching storefront in 1934, from left to right, are delivery boy Charlie Lee Marcus, Jimmy Ray Windham, Brazil Truett, Louise H. Reynolds, J. Perry Reynolds, Louise Truett, and Donnie Mae Taylor.

Prominent attorney and entrepreneur J. Monroe Spears applied his business acumen and entrepreneurial spirit to many endeavors in Lamar over the years, including editing the *Darlington Press* in 1903. Here Spears is pictured in the early 1900s inside the J. M. Spears Company textile store. From left to right are Cleo Chaplin, Emory Spears, unidentified, and J. Monroe Spears.

This is the yard of Mallie N. Gray's sawmill around 1900, near Oates, South Carolina. Oates is a crossroads community that arose after the Civil War with the opening of a general store, and later a post office, by William J. Oates (1826–1897). Pictured here from left to right are L. P. Raines, unidentified, Albert Gray, Robert Andrews, and eight unidentified.

This postcard dating from around 1910 shows the Hartsville Fertilizer Factory on Black Creek Lake, later know as Prestwood Lake. The fertilizer factory was one of Maj. James Lide Coker's entrepreneurial ventures, established in conjunction with his seed company, oil mill, and the Coker and Company General Store. Coker also founded the Southern Novelty Company in 1899, now Sonoco, which is listed as a Fortune 500 company.

Society Hill's Carolina Peach Company, chartered around 1900, was one of L. E. Carrigan's successful entrepreneurial ventures and one of the first commercial peach orchards in the state. Peach production began on a small scale in the Palmetto State in the 1850s, used chiefly for hog feed and the making of peach brandy. Production of the fruit on a large scale did not blossom in South Carolina until the 1920s. In the c. 1910 photograph above, Carolina Peach Company orchards, wagons, and farm buildings are visible. Below, juicy Carolina peaches are proudly displayed, also around 1910. The two identified subjects in the photograph are W. G. Drake, second from left, and young F. W. Drake, third from left. Peaches remain a strong agricultural product for South Carolina today.

"Frenchy" Demaurice of Darlington founded a successful jewelry business shortly after the beginning of the 20th century. This photograph of the interior of the Demaurice Jewelry Store was taken around 1921. From left to right are "Frenchy" Demaurice, an unidentified customer, and salesman Leon Flannigan. By 1970, Caper's Drugstore was located in the old jewelry store space.

The Chaplin Furniture Company furnished homes in Lamar for many years. In this *c.* 1900 photograph, (from left to right) Rowland James Chaplin, Orin Chaplin, and an unidentified gentleman pose with some of the store's modern wares.

This image is of T. A. Gandy's general store in Society Hill around 1914. The building burned in 1929. General stores of the time offered a variety of items for sale, from groceries, dry goods, and hardware to notions and candy, and were often popular gathering spots for the community.

This photograph shows the interior of Stewart's Jewelry Store in Lamar around 1915, located in the Simpson Stewart Building. The town fire truck was housed in the Simpson Stewart Building during the 1970s.

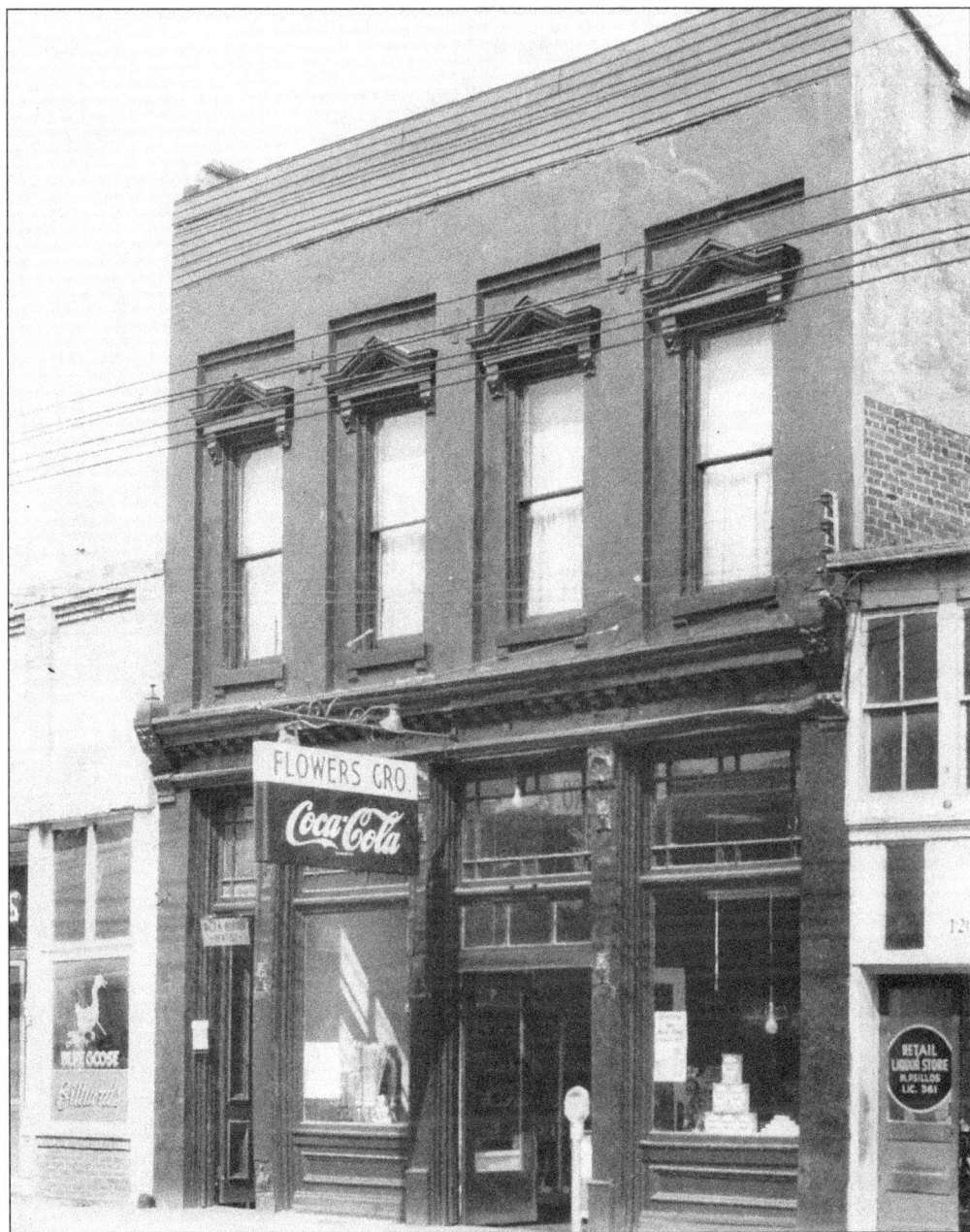

Flowers Grocery, founded by Jesse Eugene Flowers, moved into this site in the Hennig Building at 124 Pearl Street around 1930. Jesse's son, Lawrence Eugene Flowers (born 1900), took over operation of the store in 1943. This photograph was taken in 1950. Flowers Grocery closed its doors in 1953.

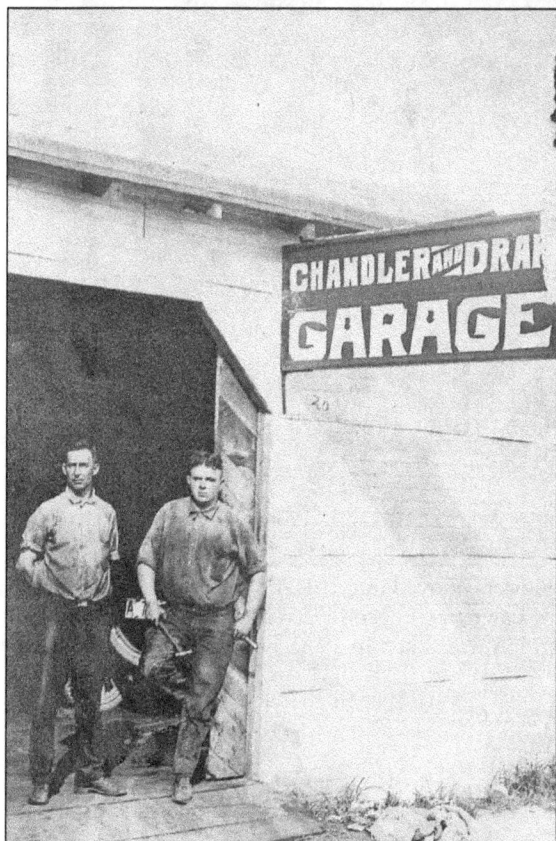

The growing popularity of the automobile prompted longtime friends Charles Chandler and Franke W. Drake to start Chandler and Drake's Garage at 251 Dargan Street in 1918. The shop was only large enough at first to house one Ford Model T, and the two mechanics soon had to enlarge to accommodate their growing business. Farmers from around the county began to bring their cars and trucks into town on Saturdays for Drake's to repair, and the crew often worked into the wee hours of the night. The c. 1918 photograph (left) shows Charles Chandler, left, and Frank W. Drake, right, ready to keep Darlington motors humming. The above picture was taken in 1920, just after the shop was made larger. From left to right are Alphonso Super, Bernice Odom, Frank Drake (with arm on chain), Carl Drake, B. F. Anderson, and Charlie Chandler. Later known as Drake's Garage, the shop continued operation well into the 1980s.

While taxicabs, once considered an undignified manner of travel, achieved iconic status in large cities by the 1930s, cab companies were a new addition in smaller towns. Donnie Porter, formerly of Pembroke, North Carolina, was one of the first entrepreneurs in the county to offer taxi service to Darlingtonians without wheels. Here Porter poses next to one of his service vehicles around 1937.

The automobiles of busy Lamar shoppers line up in front of McSween Mercantile Company, pictured in 1949. The largest and busiest department store in Lamar for years, McSween Mercantile offered the best of the last century's one-stop shopping. Shortly after the opening of McSween Mercantile in Lamar in 1911, accountant G. G. Harris of Tennessee became the bookkeeper. In 1931, Harris became co-owner of the enterprise with Lewis J. Beasley. In 1970, the building was consumed by fire, and the site became the Harris IGA.

This is J. Perry Reynolds's new general store in 1954, supplying folks in Lamar with necessities such as animal feed and groceries, perhaps accompanied by a pint of cold, delicious Buttercup ice cream and a Coca-Cola. The distinctive checkerboard design connects the new store with the old, assuring customers that Reynolds's new store offers the same exemplary selection and service.

J. K. Parrott's Society Hill grocery operated from the same location, the intersection of Main Street and Old Darlington Road across from the Welsh Neck Baptist Church, for over three decades. The surrounding scenery changed, however, and by 1950, a Gulf service station complemented Parrott's store.

90

The Temple Theatorium on South Fifth Street in Hartsville offered space upstairs for community groups to meet. One such group was the Tobacco Boosters, pictured around 1927. Tobacco production took hold in the Pee Dee region after 1900, taking the place of the failing cotton market. The Coker Pedigreed Seed Company developed hybrid tobacco plants that grew well in Southern soil.

The Darlington County Agricultural Society was established in May 1846 at Darlington Court House, with William E. James as president; I. D. Wilson, R. Campbell, and J. M. Timmons as vice presidents; W. H. Wingate as recording secretary; and William Law as treasurer. Committees were organized to study various agricultural topics and issues of importance to local planters. The improvement of cotton, barbwire versus woven wire for fencing, the cattle tick, the treatment of slaves, and the boll weevil were among topics explored. The society continues today. Celebrating a 1972 historical marker in honor of the organization are, from left to right, Lucas Dargan, Ben Williamson, David Allen, W. W. Kirven, and Robert Pitts.

Five

WORSHIP AND EDUCATION

The Welsh Neck Baptist Church of Christ is the oldest church in Darlington County, organized in 1738 by a small group of Welsh settlers on the Pee Dee River in what is now Marlboro County. Near the beginning of the 19th century, the First Great Awakening swept from the Northeast to the South, and evangelical persuasions began to take root and grow in the region. Baptist, Methodist, and Presbyterian faiths, all non-established religions, developed followers in Darlington. In 1789, Methodist missionaries arrived, and Wesley Chapel Methodist Church, first known as Gully Church, was established in the village that became Lydia around 1850. Trinity Episcopal Church was the first of its denomination in the county, organized in 1834. Scotch and Irish settlers founded the Darlington Presbyterian Church in 1827.

Another influence of the Great Awakening was a budding desire for education, reflecting not only a greater concern for the soul but also a more egalitarian perspective. In 1778, a group of Darlington District planters formed the St. David's Society and garnered resources to build St. David's Academy. A small schoolhouse about one mile from Long Bluff, the academy opened to "youths of all Christian denominations." The curriculum included lessons in Latin and Greek and attracted tutors with the best of credentials. The original building caught fire in 1813 and was rebuilt and reincarnated as the Female Benevolent Society, an all-girls school.

Prominent businessmen and planters organized the Darlington Society in 1818 to pursue educational excellence for community youth, establishing the Darlington Academy on Swift Creek. In 1860, the school took the name St. John's Academy, serving all grades from one through high school. In 1902, a three-story brick building was built to accommodate a burgeoning student body.

Welsh Neck High School opened in 1894 in Hartsville, becoming Coker College in 1908. Today Coker College, with its lovely Kalmia Gardens, remains a highly regarded educational institution in the state.

The most recent addition to Darlington's educational community is the Darlington Middle School, completed in 2007 and serving nearly 1,000 sixth- through eighth-grade students.

Verle (Mixon) Brown poses with her Sunday school class in front of the Fourth Street Baptist Church in Hartsville in 1908. The church served the mill village that surrounded the Hartsville Cotton Mill, incorporated in 1900 by Maj. James L. Coker and C. C. Twitty. Cotton bale production began in 1903, with 10,000 spindles and 350 looms, yielding 4,500 bales the first year. On the far left are, from left to right, Leo, John, and Tom Mixon. The baby held up in the back row is Carson Steen.

Soon after settling in the area granted by the British crown, the newcomers founded the Baptist Church of Christ at Welsh Neck in 1738. Plans for this beautiful church building were drawn in 1840 and completed in 1843. The view in this photograph is of the front of the church; the steeple is at the back, an uncommon architectural feature. In 1928, the original Welsh Neck Baptist Church was struck by lightning and burned to the ground.

This wonderful old two-story Southern home, built in 1858, was the parsonage for the Welsh Neck Baptist Church in Society Hill for many years. It is not known when this photograph was taken.

This image is the old Welsh Neck Baptist Cemetery around 1900. Victorian cemeteries exhibited a great deal of symbolism, either through statuary or engravings on the tombstones.

This photograph reveals the interior of the 1843 Welsh Neck Baptist Church decorated for a wedding around 1915. The greenery and flowers would have all been fresh, an important part of an early-20th-century wedding. Church weddings were not standard. Until this time, wedding ceremonies were most often held in private homes.

In 1916, when this photograph was taken of young people participating in Confederate Memorial Day services on the steps of the Welsh Neck Baptist Church, it was a solemn occasion in honor of fallen soldiers. Just around 50 years had passed since the Civil War devastated the South, and the memories of the men who lost their lives were still fresh in many minds.

This undated photograph, taken next to the Welsh Neck Baptist Church Baptistery, shows, from left to right, Jim Blackman, Jane Carrigan, Ann Sompayrac, Frances Guy, and Buddy Guy.

Newman Swamp Methodist Church evolved in the early 1800s from Windham's Meeting House, a venue for itinerant circuit-riding preachers. The church offered a school for children in Lamar for many decades. Here the young 1926 class of teacher Willie Pollard of the Newman Swamp School poses engagingly for the camera. From left to right are (first row) Elma Watford, Bessie Amerson, Asa Windham, Melissa Watford, unidentified, Alvis Sy Howell, Mitchell Howell, unidentified, and E. J. Clements; (second row) Alma Windham, Sarah Watford, Grace Windham, Cuyler Fields, and Ulysses Bell.

The Society Hill Presbyterian Church was erected in 1891, and like most historic buildings, it underwent many additions and changes over time. This photograph is an early image of the church, probably captured around 1900.

Trinity Episcopal Protestant Church in Society Hill, founded in 1834, was the first Episcopal church in Darlington County. By 1930, the church stopped offering regular services, but it has opened its doors for one annual service every year since 1969, courtesy of St. Matthew's Episcopal Church in Darlington. The road in front of Trinity Episcopal remained unpaved, as it had always been, until around 1960.

The Swift Creek Baptist Church originated in 1844. This photograph shows the church in 1903, just after completion of the new building. In 1950, a brick church was built nearby, and this building was demolished.

The Swift Creek Baptist Church, completed in 1903, hosted a wedding in style and elegance on December 26, 1936, joining in matrimony Darlington County schoolteacher Alice Lee with lawyer James Woodrow Lewis, later to become the Honorable Chief Justice J. Woodrow Lewis of the South Carolina Supreme Court. A local newspaper reported that "beautiful in its dignity and simplicity . . . against a backdrop of pines, Southern smilax and lighted candles the bridal party made a picture of distinctive beauty."

The St. David's Society formed in 1777 in Long Bluff to create an academy for the education of community youth. After the Revolutionary War, the plan reached fruition, and St. David's Academy opened its doors to the first class in October 1786. Here students of all ages and faculty stand outside the schoolhouse around 1898.

St. David's Academy underwent numerous reincarnations over the years because of fire, increased enrollment, or modernization. The first rebuilding occurred in 1813, when the original building burned and was replaced immediately. This image shows the academy around 1910, after a second story added to the original first floor allowed the school to expand.

Ashton Gandy, left, and Horace Rudisill chat at the annual Trinity Episcopal Homecoming, May 19, 1991, in Society Hill.

In 1818, the Darlington Society raised the funds to build a schoolhouse on Swift Creek, the Darlington Academy, which became known as St. John's around mid-century. In 1902, St. John's Academy, serving all grades through high school, expanded into a new brick building. However, enrollment continued to increase, and by 1915, a separate high school building was constructed. Here St. John's football team of 1916 displays its grit. From left to right are (first row) Francis Byrd, Ernest Pearle, McIver Edwards, Joe Keyes Baird, Robert E. James, and Evander Brown; (second row) George Brown, Oliver Kullock, Alston McKeithan, Bill Hursey, Hewitt Fulton, unidentified, and the coach.

From the Darlington Academy of the early 1800s to Hartsville's Welsh Neck High School and its subsequent transformation into Coker College of today, Darlington County has valued education. This photograph from the Darlington County Teacher's Conference held at St. John's Academy in 1902 shows many of the county's dedicated teachers. Superintendent Henry C. Burn, third row on the far left, poses with the schoolteachers of Darlington County. Teachers identified are Sallie Howle, fourth from right, back row; Ann McIver, first row, far left; and Carrie McIver, fourth from left in the third row from the back with head tilted.

These Jasper School children, hats in hand, mug for the camera in front of the Jasper School around 1900. Jasper is located in the lower part of Darlington County near Florence, and like many small communities, it grew up at a crossroads.

This was the newly completed, two-story Swift Creek School with the entire student body and teachers in 1905. A consolidation of three community schools, this building was utilized until 1921, when the ever-growing population of Swift Creek required yet a larger structure.

Three small schools in the community of Antioch, outside of Hartsville, joined in 1914 to attend the new Antioch Industrial School. The school, pictured here around 1918, cost more than $15,000 to build, and with its coat of red paint, it was considered state-of-the-art in institutional design. Antioch Industrial School closed in the 1950s, and an elementary school was constructed on the grounds. Antioch High School students attended Hartsville High School.

Here, in the foreground from left to right, are James F. Ousley and Marion Ousley; in the background are Rev. Thomas Henderson, with coat blowing, George McIntosh, and Charlie Griggs in front of the Antioch High School in 1915. The Antioch School was one of the first "industrial" schools in the state, offering classes in home economics for girls and basic industrial skills for boys, such as carpentry and masonry.

The Hartsville High School class of 1913 poses solemnly for a picture. From left to right are (first row) Annie Lou Erwin, Ruby Rogers, Beatrice Lee, and unidentified; (second row) Henry McLeod, Charles H. Ellis Jr., Carroll Deschamps, Alva Tarte, and Thomas Burns; (third row) Sallie Beard, Grace Lee, unidentified, and Bessie McNair. The current Hartsville High School, built in 1961, continues a tradition of exemplary education. In January 2008, the school became the first in the Darlington County School District to offer the prestigious International Baccalaureate college preparatory program.

Hartsville High School, established in the early 1900s, has long been praised for excellence in athletics and music. Today Hartsville High, led by Principal Dr. Charlie Burry, serves around 1,400 students in grades 9 through 12. Here in the 1970s, the Hartsville High School Band proudly leads a parade down Carolina Avenue. Note the sign for Coker's Pedigreed Seed, a company created by David R. Coker in 1913.

Six

FESTIVALS, OCCASIONS, AND ASSOCIATIONS

Festivals and fairs are an extension of community pride and spirit, offering food and fun as well as education and public relations for local merchants, agriculture, and industry. Such occasions celebrate the heritage of towns and neighborhoods and deepen community ties. Closely related are ceremonies honoring or commemorating special events, such as Darlington County's bicentennial celebration in 1972 or the tribute to Darlington-born jazz musicians Buddy and Ella Johnson in 2002. Some observances are filled with sorrow, such as those in memory of fallen soldiers in the many wars involving Darlingtonians since the American Revolution.

Associations and societies function in a variety of ways as well. The Darlington District Agricultural Society, formed by John Hart in 1846, promoted progressive farming practices to mid-19th-century planters. In addition to establishing an experimental farm in the late 1880s, Hart is credited with installing the mule in Southern agriculture. The society was an ardent promoter of the annual Darlington Fair, debuting in 1871 and continuing for 20 years.

Scottish and English Freemasons in Darlington organized St. Alban's Masonic Lodge in the early 1820s, offering fraternity, charity functions, and entertainment and staging gala balls for the entertainment of the entire community. Other groups of note over the centuries include the Damon Gun Club, dating from the late 1800s; the Hartsville Rotary Club of South Carolina; and the Darlington Kiwanis Club.

Through the brotherhood and solidarity of groups from the African American Bricklayer's Association, organized around 1900, to women's social and service clubs such as the Over the Teacups Club, spanning generations from 1899 until 1949, Darlington County demonstrates a rich and diverse network of social and labor-related organizations.

Today visitors to Darlington County enjoy the Lamar Egg Scramble each spring, an annual Jazz! Carolina affair in Hartsville, the South Carolina Sweet Potato Festival in Darlington, the RenoFest Bluegrass Festival in downtown Hartsville every March, and the Society Hill Catfish Festival, presented in the fall.

The Knights of Pythias is a fraternal organization founded in Washington, D.C., in 1864. The order was inspired by an Irish poet's play about Damon and Pythias and revolves around loyalty, honor, and friendship. This photograph of the Hartsville lodge of the Knights of Pythias dates from around 1900. F. A. Miller is the third knight from the left in the second row. Other notable organization members over the years include Abraham Lincoln, William Jennings Bryan, Nelson A. Rockefeller, and Franklin D. Roosevelt.

The Darlington Dramatic Club performed in the old opera house located in Morehead's Loft across from the Darlington Bank on the corner of the square. Several of the thespians pictured in this image had recently come from Scotland, such as J. L. Michie. The group's first presentation was *Nevada*, a western drama. A later production of *Mikado* proved so successful they took it on the road, giving performances in the nearby towns of Cheraw, Sumter, and Bennettsville. From left to right are (first row) Carrie McIver, Dr. Will J. Garner, and Emma Williamson; (second row) J. L. Michie, George M. Boyd, Gen. W. E. James, Frank D. Spain, Catsie Spain, Col. Henry Thompson, and Thomas H. Spain.

Darlington County horse enthusiasts formed the Darlington Driving Association in the 1890s, building a racetrack at Doneraile for highly anticipated competitions. Note the size of the crowd that turned out for this race event around 1900.

The Darlington Driving Association also organized an annual horse show, held on the Darlington square every year on the Fourth of July from the early 1900s through World War I. This image shows people gathering on the west side of the square for the 1907 festivities, and several shops are decorated for the event. Whittington's Drugstore in the left corner of the photograph was built in 1892 and remained a drugstore until 1983.

Two Darlington County ladies dressed for the occasion claim a strategic spot on the square from which to view the Fourth of July horse show activities in 1913, most likely awaiting a couple of gentlemen bearing a picnic.

The Colonial Dames of America, founded in 1890, is an organization of women descended from British-American ancestors between 1607 and 1775 who were of service to the colonies. Here are Hartsville's Colonial Dames, pictured around 1945 before a special event. From left to right are (first row) Ruth Burch, Amelia Sojourner, and Helen Zeigler; (second row) Frances Johnson, Ivey Schofoeld, Julia Hicks, Cora Smith, Flora Mae McLeod, Elizabeth Stikeleather, and Mary Foster Brunson.

A gun club existed in Darlington before E. O. Damon purchased land on the Pee Dee in the 1890s, when the preserve became known as Damon Swamp. Damon, a skilled hunter and taxidermist, carried on with tradition. Today the annual Damon Gun Club Hunt draws hundreds of marksmen, their friends, and family for a Thanksgiving feast in the clubhouse. Gen. Wade Hampton is reputed to have hunted alongside gun club members in the early years before 1900. The above image shows the original clubhouse built by Damon around 1895. The picture below, around 1898, illustrates a bountiful day.

Women's clubs and societies from the Progressive Era into the 20th century served to ease women into the public sphere through self-education, self-improvement, and the promotion of libraries and children's educational programs. From 1899 to 1949, Darlington's Over the Teacups Club studied Southern and South Carolina state history. Over the years, the club read classic histories of the Civil War as well as works by Southern women, such as Mary Chesnut's *Diary from Dixie*. The top photograph, taken in the library of Mrs. Bright Williamson's house on Oak Street around 1950, shows, from left to right, (seated on the sofa) Mrs. C. W. Milling, Mrs. Clarence McCall, and Mrs. Bright Williamson; (around the room) Mrs. M. L. Coggeshall, Mrs. B. Franklin Williamson, Mrs. A. L. James, Mrs. T. Dudley Paulling, Mrs. R. E. James Jr., Mrs. R. W. Coggeshall, Mrs. T. E. Wilson, Mrs. W. E. James, Mrs. J. C. Daniel, Mrs. Wiley Rhodes, Mrs. A. J. Howard Jr., Mrs. E. C. Dennis, and Mrs. James Edwards. The bottom photograph was taken on the club's 50th anniversary celebration in 1949. From left to right are Lucretia McKey, Jessie Coggeshall Rogers, Marion Coggeshall, Evans Wilson, Lavinia Coker Rogers, Eugene McCown, Mrs. J. R. Coggeshall (Carrie), Mrs. M. L. Coggeshall (Jessie), and Mrs. Albert James (Xina).

The Boy Scouts of America were founded in 1910, and Darlington County formed a local chapter soon after. Here is Scoutmaster Rev. O. T. Porcher's well-outfitted group in 1914. From left to right are (first row) ? Jolly, Percy Lamotte, Joe Keyes Beard, Ino T. Langston, Ted Coggeshall, R. T. Kern, and Preston Edwards; (second row) Newton Harrell, Frank Williamson, Tom Buchanan, William S. Hoole, William Boatwright, ? Dufft, William Haynesworth, Chap Milling, and Eugene Vaughan; (third row) Jay Buchanan, Fraser Evans, Don Michie, Roger S. Wells, Kendall Evans, Harold Norment, William Norment, and George Patton. Scoutmaster Porcher stands on the right.

It was good fun—and good for business, too—to participate in local parades. The Daniel Lumber Company, owned by Darlington's Brunson family, spent a lot of time creating a spectacular float for one of Darlington's parades. This photograph was taken in the 1940s, when mules were still a common sight around town.

The Prestwood Country Club in Hartsville was established around 1915. Club founders included A. L. M. Wiggins, Warren Arthur, William H. Sory, and Gus A. Kalber. These ladies pose on the pier in front of the original wooden clubhouse on Prestwood Lake. A new clubhouse replaced this one in the mid-1920s.

Here a group of Hartsville's Prestwood Country Club golfers and their caddies pose for a snapshot on the green around 1935. Standing from left to right are Bobby Spence, Rankin Sowell, Glenn Lawhon Sr., Odell Duckett, Bob McKorrell, Joseph Haun, Robert Coker, Gus Kalber, Dr. William Byerly Sr., J. B. Blackmon, Charles Manship, Crawford Timberlake, Howard Gandy, "Doc" Arthur, John Stephenson, and William "Willie" Sory. Caddies seated in the first row are unidentified.

The Darlington Kiwanis Club, chartered in 1921 with 51 original members, is shown here on the steps of the McFall Hotel in 1922. The front rows include J. F. Pate, C. E. Sligh, W. H. McFall, J. Lester Perkins, Dr. G. B. Edwards, C. Rogers Wells, G. H. Brown, ? Finklea, Ben Hilb, J. E. Moncrief, E. C. Pendergast, A. P. Mozingo, and D. T. McKeithan Jr. In the middle row are Rev. J. H. Grave, J. R. Kilgo, A. M. Hill, J. M. Napier, Arthur Blackwell, Marion Bonnoitt, Bright Williamson, Russell Acree, T. H. Lever, and unidentified. From left to right, in the back two rows, loosely, are Dr. C. C. Hill, Judge E. C. Dennis, Audley Howard, R. W. Welling, W. F. Twitty, L. A. Langston, W. H. Bristow, P. J. Boatwright, Rev. D. M. Fulton, Ervin Welling, C. M. Ward, J. K. Doyle, T. O. Simmons, unidentified, T. Miller White, R. E. James, unidentified, D. A. Cohen, Monroe Hill, Rev. F. W Putney, Allen Bonnoitt (in bow tie), John T. Langston (behind Bonnoitt), and J. T. Stanley.

Here is the first Darlington American Legion Junior baseball team, hoping for good luck in a big game in 1927. Included here are F. T. Siskron (left foreground with the ball cap) Bob Lumiansky, Hugh Colmin, Richard Davis, Edward Welch, Richard Vaughan, John Brown, Roland Tew, John Corbett Troutman, Booth Ward, and Frank Clifton.

The Hartsville Rotary Club of South Carolina was established in 1942. Rotary Clubs are an international organization of service clubs with the goal of combining business and professional leaders to provide humanitarian service and to spread goodwill and peace. Meetings are weekly social gatherings to organize community and international service projects. This is the Hartsville Rotary Club in 1942. From left to right are (first row) Vance Tatum, Carroll Jordan, Hal Manda, Charles Denny, F. C. Chitty, Vernon Fagan, D. L. White, and H. P. Southerland; (second row) Anthony Lawrence, Dr. J. E. Mills, J. K. Taylor, F. C. Huff, Jones Ellison, W. D. Arthur, F. E. Fitchett, Colon Segars, John Stephenson, J. B. Blackmon, L. H. Stukes, J. B. Redfearn, Bill Eggleston, J. B. Gilbert, "Punk" Jackson, and Leon Pennington.

George Lindsay, also known as Goober Pyle in the 1960s television sitcom *The Andy Griffith Show*, is the guest of honor at the Southern 500 festivities in 1969. A number of celebrities and notables attended the popular parade, held in Darlington each Saturday before Labor Day for more than 30 years.

A beauty contest was an integral part of Southern 500 festivities every year. Lovely and talented young women from all over the Palmetto State competed each Labor Day weekend to be crowned Miss Southern 500. In this photograph in 1971, Susan Gordon, the previous year's queen, crowns Nancy Mitchum the new Miss Southern 500.

State agencies joined in Southern 500 parade celebrations, spreading their own public service messages. This early-1970s parade entry from the Alcohol, Tobacco, and Firearms division of the U.S. Treasury Department educates parade goers on the dangers of smoking, guns, and an old Southern tradition, moonshine. Below, in 1970, the Southern 500 parade judges await the show on their stand in the Darlington square in front of the Darlington courthouse, built in 1965.

Darlington County's bicentennial celebration was a momentous occasion. Over 3,000 people turned out in Lamar to watch the bicentennial parade and participate in festivities in 1972. Here people gather early in the day, many dressed in period garb, to hear welcoming speeches.

In this photograph, Horace Rudisill stands at the intersection of Main Street and Railroad Avenue in Lamar addressing celebrants at the 1972 bicentennial celebration. Rudisill's speech drew one of the celebration's largest crowds. A well-known historian in the community, Rudisill spent many years collecting documents, images, and oral histories of Darlington County, working tirelessly to house the collection in the Darlington County Historical Commission archives.

BIBLIOGRAPHY

Bierer, Bert W. *Discovering South Carolina*. Columbia, SC: The State Printing Company, 1969.

Darlington News and Press, Darlington, SC, 1874–2007.

Edgar, Walter. *South Carolina: A History*. Columbia, SC: University of South Carolina Press, 1998.

Ervin, Eliza Cowan, and Horace Fraser Rudisill, eds. *Darlingtoniana: A History of People, Places and Events in Darlington County, South Carolina*. Spartanburg, SC: The Reprint Company, 1997.

Gregg, Alexander. *History of the Old Cheraws*. New York: Richardson and Company, 1867.

Guess, William F. *South Carolina: Annals of Pride and Protest*. New York: Harper, 1960.

Hartsville Museum, ed. *Milestones: Hartsville Centennial, 1891–1991: Centennial Histories of Hartsville*, 2nd ed. Hartsville, SC: History Committee, 2000.

Hooker, Richard J., ed. *The Carolina Backcountry on the Eve of Revolution: The Journal and Other Writings of Charles Woodmason, Anglican Itinerant*. Chapel Hill, NC: University of North Carolina Press, 1953.

The Messenger, Hartsville, SC, 1893–2007.

Milling, Chapman J. *Red Carolinians*. Columbia, SC: University of South Carolina Press, 1969.

Rudisill, Horace Fraser. *Darlington County: A Pictorial History: From the Photographic Archives of the Darlington County Historical Commission*, 2nd ed. Virginia Beach, VA: The Donning Company, 2007.

Weir, Robert. *Colonial South Carolina: A History*. Columbia, SC: University of South Carolina Press, 1997.

Visit us at
arcadiapublishing.com

....

www.ingramcontent.com/pod-product-compliance
Lightning Source LLC
Chambersburg PA
CBHW080617110426
42813CB00006B/1536